IVANKA TRUMP

THE

TRUMP CARD

PLAYING TO WIN IN WORK AND LIFE

A TOUCHSTONE BOOK
PUBLISHED BY SIMON & SCHUSTER

NEW YORK   LONDON   TORONTO   SYDNEY

Touchstone
A Division of Simon & Schuster, Inc.
1230 Avenue of the Americas
New York, NY 10020

Copyright © 2009 by Ivanka Trump

All rights reserved, including the right to reproduce this book or portions thereof in any form whatsoever. For information address Touchstone Subsidiary Rights Department, 1230 Avenue of the Americas, New York, NY 10020.

First Touchstone trade paperback edition April 2010

TOUCHSTONE and colophon are registered trademarks of Simon & Schuster, Inc.

For information about special discounts for bulk purchases, please contact Simon & Schuster Special Sales at 1-866-506-1949 or business@simonandschuster.com.

The Simon & Schuster Speakers Bureau can bring authors to your live event. For more information or to book an event contact the Simon & Schuster Speakers Bureau at 1-866-248-3049 or visit our website at www.simonspeakers.com.

Designed by Ruth Lee-Mui

Manufactured in the United States of America

4   6   8   10   9   7   5

Library of Congress Cataloging-in-Publication Data

Trump, Ivanka.
The Trump card : playing to win in work and life
/ Ivanka Trump—1st ed.
p. cm.
"A Touchstone Book."
1. Success in business.   2. Success—Psychological aspects.
3. Trump, Ivanka, 1981–   I. Title.
HF5386.T81495 2009
650.1—dc22   2009024563

ISBN 978-1-4391-4001-7
ISBN 978-1-4391-4015-4 (pbk)
ISBN 978-1-4391-5564-6 (ebook)

To Mom and Dad:

Your support has been endless. Thank you for paving the way and setting an example for me and my brothers in both work and life.

To Don and Eric:

My favorite "colleagues" and best friends. I love you both very much.

To Tiffany and Barron:

The next generation . . . I know that you will make us proud!

To Dorothy Curry and Babi:

Thanks for offering me your shoulders, and your home cooking, when I needed it most.

To Melania:

Thank you for your continued support and encouragement.

To Mel Berger, Dan Paisner, Zachary Schisgal, Trish Todd, and Chris Morrow:

Thank you for helping me make this book happen.

In honor of Bridget Carroll, Dedo, Grandpa Fred, and Grandma Mary. I miss you.

If you do work that you love, and the work fulfills you, the rest will come.

—OPRAH WINFREY

CONTENTS

THE
TRUMP CARD

INTRODUCTION:

GET OVER IT

You can't build a reputation on what you are going to do.
—HENRY FORD

In business, as in life, nothing is ever handed to you.

That might sound like a line coming from someone with a backstory like mine—and a load!—but if you know me and my family, you'll understand that I come by these words honestly. Yes, I've had the great good fortune to be born into a life of wealth and privilege, with a name to match. Yes, I've had every opportunity, every advantage. And yes, I've chosen to build my career on a foundation built by my father and grandfather, so I can certainly see why an outsider might dismiss my success in our family business as yet another example of nepotism.

But my parents set the bar high for me and my brothers. They gave us a lot, it's true, but they expected a lot in return. And you can be sure we didn't rise to our positions in the company by any kind of birthright or foregone conclusion. My father is definitely not the kind of guy who'd place his children in key roles within his organization if he didn't think we could surpass the expectations he had for us. You see, in the Trump household, it was never just about meeting the expectations of others. It was about exceeding them. It was about surprising people. And being the best. Anything less was second-rate,

1

which probably explains one of my biggest worries starting out—that I would merely be competent at my job in the Trump Organization. Good enough, and nothing more.

I can still remember how anxious I felt, how completely out of my element, when I was appointed to the board of directors of Trump Entertainment Resorts, the parent corporation of our casino operations in Atlantic City. Realize, this was no closely held family business. It was a public company, so there was enormous pressure to prove that I belonged. Some of that pressure was real, and some of it was imagined—but that didn't make it any less terrifying. I can still remember walking over to my first board meeting at the law offices of Weil, Gotshal & Manges, feeling incredibly nervous the whole way. It was just a five-minute walk, but that was more than enough time to think through every worst-case scenario. It didn't help that just before I left my office someone pointed out that I was about to become the youngest director on the board of a publicly traded company in the United States; I had enough to worry about already. I was twenty-five years old, just a year or so into my tenure at Trump, about to sit around a conference table with a group of middle-aged men—some of whom, I'm sure, would be wondering what the hell I was doing there. On some level I knew that I'd been tapped to represent the voice of a younger generation and to represent my family's interests in the company that bore our brand. But on another, I worried that I'd be exposed as a kid in over her head. My formal appointment was still subject to board approval, and I still had to apply for a gaming license and gain other clearances, but I vowed on that uneasy walk that I would never give these people a reason to question the value I brought to the table.

The whole way over to that meeting, it felt to me as if my appointment to the board was stacked all the way against me: I was young and inexperienced; I was a woman; and I was Donald Trump's daughter. (It might appear as if this last would be a plus, but I didn't see it counting for a whole lot in my favor; if anything, it might have given the impression that I had been tapped only for some vague public relations value.) Growing up with two brothers, I'd watched enough base-ball to know that you get only three strikes, so I might have counted myself out before I even stepped to the plate. But then I realized that what some people might regard as a negative, others might see as a strength. Maybe my relative youth and inexperience would help me offer a fresh take. Maybe the board needed a young woman's perspec-tive. Maybe the fact that I was Donald Trump's eyes and ears on the board, as I was at the Trump Organization and on his reality television show, would make me uniquely qualified to offer insights and strate-gies for positioning the three Trump-branded casinos that were the primary assets of the company.

In any case, it was overwhelming. Intimidating. So how did I han-dle it? I dug in, breathed deep, and vowed to do whatever it took to show my new colleagues on the board and the company's manage-ment team that I added real value. And merely belonging wouldn't quite cut it, in my estimation. I was determined to play an integral role. I might be nervous, but I wouldn't show it. I might be intimi-dated, but I wouldn't show it. I might even be a bit overmatched, in my first few meetings, but I'd get up to speed before long. And sure enough, that's just what happened. By the end of that first meeting, most of my anxieties fell away, and I walked back to my office in Trump Tower feeling as if I had made a contribution, after all. As if I would make an even greater contribution going forward.

Let's face it, when you come from a place where *good enough* is not quite good enough, you're bound to push yourself. You're disinclined to take anything for granted. And you're not about to be dismissed just because someone might think you've had an unfair advantage. These days, I try not to let it bother me when someone jumps to conclusions about my abilities. I have a tough skin and enough confidence not to worry too much about being underestimated because of my last name, my relative youth, or my modeling background. It comes with the ter-ritory. I've reached the point where I know I'm no lightweight. I'm perfectly capable of separating my colleagues and associates from this type of snap judgment when it comes up—which happens less and less these days, I'm happy to report.

The message I put out to people who are prepared to write me off before even meeting with me: get over it. It's the same message I used to give to myself whenever I spent too much time worrying what people would think of me or how I'd risen to my position in the company or what attributes I brought to the table. I'd catch myself agonizing along these lines and think, Just get over it, Ivanka. Or, It's not your problem, it's theirs. After all, I eventually realized, we've all got our own baggage. Whatever we do, whatever our backgrounds, we've all had some kind of advantage somewhere along the way. Some break that might have gone to someone else. Some edge or inside track we couldn't have counted on.

CONSIDER THE STAGGER

As long as I'm on that inside track, I might as well work that metaphor a bit more to make my point. That perceived lead I might have had starting out? It's like the stagger you see in a middle-distance event at a track meet. You know, where the runners line up in a stepping-stone way in their separate lanes, the runner in the outside lane well ahead of the field before the starting gun goes off, the runner in the inside lane well behind. It's set up that way so that each runner covers the same ground before she reaches the first straightaway, but it has the appearance of being an advantage. In truth, the only advantage is psychological; each runner ends up covering the same ground by the end of the race. With me, it probably looked as if I were in the outside lane, way ahead of the rest of the pack before the race even started. But I still had to run the distance. I still had to go to school, learn the basics, develop my own style, make and support my own decisions, and on and on.

What a lot of people don't realize is that this all-too-common misperception usually runs hand in hand with another. It took me a while to recognize this, but there's definitely a flip side to how other people might see you, way out there in life's outer lane with that apparent jump start. On the one hand, you get the idea that my success is purely a by-product of privilege, proximity, or favoritism—or, relatedly, that Donald Trump's daughter could not possibly have ascended to the role of vice president of his real estate company for any reason but filial devotion. People assume that I'm not smart enough or driven enough or savvy enough to have made it on my own. On the other, it's just the opposite. People build it up in their heads that just because I'm Donald Trump's daughter, it must mean I have an inherent understanding of all things related to real estate and finance.

(I guess it could be worse!)

I used to get this a lot when I was at Wharton, as an undergraduate at the University of Pennsylvania, where my classmates would turn to me whenever a professor posted a challenging question. In their minds, because I'd spent so much time with my father and shared the same genes and mind-set, I must know the answer automatically. And truth be told, I still get this kind of deferential treatment. People sometimes approach me tentatively or suspiciously because of my father's reputation as a world-class negotiator, as if they think I'm about to take advantage of them. As if I know something I'm not letting on. It can be a big disadvantage, especially going into a negotiation, when I'd much rather be *underestimated.* My brothers tell me that the same thing happens to them all the time, so we just deal with it and move on.

I get it from both sides, the good and the bad. Positive and negative. And I've learned to ignore it. To rise above it. I refuse to let the opinions of others define how I see myself, how I carry myself, how I get through my days. It's just not relevant to me. If I got upset every time someone suggested that I was coasting on my last name, my looks, or the silver spoon that might or might not have been lodged in my mouth at birth, I'd be a basket case. And if I pumped myself up and found an ego shot in every tossed-off bit of undeserved praise, my head would be too big to get through my office door.

And so: get over it. Go ahead and bring it up if you feel you must. Acknowledge the elephant in the room. But then move on. Move on, because I'm way past it. Move on, because even though those who believe that my success is a result of nepotism might be right, they might also be wrong. Try as I may—and try as my critics may—there's just no way to measure the advantage I've gained from having the Trump name, just as there's no way to know if the person sitting across from you in a job interview or a negotiation is there on his or her own merits or with an assist of one kind or other.

What I do know is this: I'm incredibly and endlessly proud of what my family has accomplished. It starts with my father, I suppose— but then, he'd probably tell you it starts with *his* father, my grandfather. And there's also my mother to factor in. She's played a big role in my development as a businesswoman: her strength, her discipline, her character. (She'd probably put some of *that* on her parents as well.) My brothers, too, have had a hand in my success, just as I hope I've had a hand in theirs. I've come to realize that we bring something to one another, so that the whole is greater than the sum of its parts. We're a wellspring of individual talents and perspectives, and I drink from it all. *We* drink from it all. So rather than worrying about what other people think or how they calibrate or credit our attributes and achievements, my focus is to ensure that these successes continue for the next generation of Trumps. After all, we Trumps don't play to perceptions. We play to win.

Gosh, I sound like my father, don't I? But that's what you get from this particular Daddy's girl.

PLAYING YOUR "TRUMP" CARD

The perceived edge, the *stagger*, the loaded or backhanded compliments, the unearned deferential treatment—it all takes me in a roundabout way to the book you now hold in your hands, a business memoir, shot through with life lessons and hard-won insights for young women looking to jump-start their own careers. Yes, from the pen of a former model. Yes, from an entrepreneur who's built her reputation on her family name—in the family business, no less. But you can't judge a book by its cover, right? There's a reason the phrase has become a cliché: it's true. Okay, so I've had a bit of an edge getting in the door, but that doesn't mean I haven't developed an edge of my own now that I'm all the way in the room.

A word, first, on the title: *The Trump Card.* It's meant to signal that we've all been dealt a winning hand and that it's up to each of us to play it right and smart. In bridge, of course, the trump card is the one that prevails, no matter what, and as a strategy it's usually held in reserve for when it's most needed. I've played it here because I like the metaphor and the way it shows how I've tried to play my own winning hand.

Lately, I've been playing that hand in a family business that would be all but unrecognizable to my grandfather, who started out building and operating affordable rental housing in the New York City boroughs of Brooklyn, Queens, and Staten Island in the 1930s. Now, as executive vice president in the Trump Organization, I'm on the front lines of such seismic change at our company that even I don't recognize the offices I used to visit every day after school. Already I've played an integral role in developing more than seventy real estate projects around the world, including buildings in New York, Chicago, and Dubai. That role has very little to do with who my grandfather was or who my father is and quite a lot to do with what I've learned along the way. At one point, I might have been in just a bit over my head and pushed along before I was ready, but now my days are filled with meetings and decisions and prospects. I might talk over a potential branding deal with a developer in Indonesia in the morning and just a few hours later visit a construction site to negotiate price with a concrete contractor from the Bronx. I'll sit down at a conference table with a group of bankers and lawyers to work out the financing for a new hotel, then return to the same table six months later with a group of architects and interior designers to define what that hotel will actually look like. I once flew to South America to meet with a developer and then spent several tense days negotiating the terms of a partnership relating to a 2.6-million-square-foot property, coming home with a deal my father called one of the best he'd ever seen. Or I'll work with my jewelry design team to put the finishing touches on a magnificent new collection.

No one day is like another, and they've all added up to a wealth of experience. *My* experience. I've been exposed to a level of responsibility that's very rare for someone my age. *My* responsibility. While most young people in business spend their twenties enduring the growing pains and lowly paper-pushing assignments that come with earning your stripes, I've been able to bypass (mostly) that sort of grunt work and have been part of upper management from very early in my career.

Have I had an advantage? Absolutely. Have I safeguarded the trump card I've been dealt in my winning hand for when I needed it the most? Again, absolutely. Does that mean I can't play that card or build on those advantages and take away some insights and strategies that might help other would-be entrepreneurs from gaining an edge of their own? Absolutely not. In fact, one of the biggest advantages has come in a once-removed sort of way, and I hope to pass it along in these pages. You see, I've had tremendous access to some of the most creative, freethinking minds in business—much of it thanks to my parents' friends and associates. But contacts are only that. A point of connection. A place to start. It's what you do with those contacts that counts, and here I've tried to take what these accomplished people have given—sometimes freely, sometimes grudgingly—and then ask for a little bit more besides. I've learned firsthand from some of the most successful people on the planet, in all walks of life.

Over the years, so many remarkable people have taken the time to answer my questions and share their philosophies with me, and not just the boldface, CEO-type names. I've learned just as much from equally impressive and influential people who operate under the public radar. I take every opportunity I can to talk with these market leaders, the hardworking, hard-charging people who've been over some of the same roads I'm looking to travel, so I can see how their minds work and recognize the traits we have in common as well as where we differ. In the end, it's what we can glean from our mentors, role models, and fleeting acquaintances that sets us apart.

So I'll include some of these strategies in these pages, to reinforce the critical point that we learn not just by doing but by listening in on and reaching out to the successful people we meet in our lives, to learn what we can from their struggles and their triumphs. You'll hear from some of my most influential and innovative friends and contacts in between chapters in segments I'm calling "Bulletins from My Black-Berry," for the way it reminds us that these points of connection are available to all of us. Hopefully, these shared insights will offer you a feel for what it's like to be on the receiving end of so many powerful lessons from so many inspiring individuals—and the encouragement and inspiration to access the authoritative viewpoints within reach in your own lives.

The message I take in from the people who inspire me is that success isn't something that happens to you; you happen to it. Confidence is key, and there was always plenty of that to go around in our house. Forget the silver spoon and the storybook upbringing. This is the single most important asset I've inherited from my parents: confidence. (Perseverance runs a close second, by the way.) Without it, I couldn't work as a developer in a field dominated by older men. And without it, I couldn't have launched a jewelry business in such an uncertain economic climate.

Did I grow up with every advantage? Well, maybe not *every* advantage but some. Did I have an edge, getting started in business? No question. But get over it. And read on. Together, we'll figure out a way to hold onto the trump cards we've been dealt until we can put them to the best possible use.

WHY A BOOK?

I'm fully aware of the favorable hand I've drawn in life. And profoundly grateful for it. I also get that there's something inherently condescending about any twenty-seven-year-old trying to give people advice—especially this particular twenty-seven-year-old, who still has so much to learn. It doesn't matter how many deals I've done or how many captains of industry I can get to return my phone calls. I'm still just a couple of years out of school, still just a couple of years into my career. But that's precisely the point. We young guns have a lot to offer one another in a comparing-notes sort of way. When I reach for a book to help me past a hurdle or two in my business life, I don't go looking for a dry manual written by some sixty-year-old male, reflecting on a long career. I want to hear from someone who still knows what it was like to stay up all night cramming for an exam. Who can still taste the anxiety of speaking up for the first time in a big meeting. Who still gets goose bumps when she opens a box of new business cards after her first promotion. Who finds her way to the office on a Sunday morning after being out half the night dancing with her friends.

Like it or not, that's me. Believe it or not, that's me. Despite my title, my pedigree, and my responsibilities, I'm just like any other young woman in the workplace. I question my role in life. I struggle to find the right balance between work and play. I go to the movies or out with my friends, but I also make my work a priority. And even though I think I'm close to getting it right, I'm still searching for a style that's appropriate for someone in my professional position, a style that expresses my spirit and sass and seriousness all at once. Basically, I'm looking for the same things as a lot of young women just starting out in business—and, trust me, we're not only deferring to wizened old boardroom veterans for advice on what to wear to work, how to prepare for a key meeting, or when to seize an opportunity. We're looking to one another, just as we might have reached out to a friend from home who was a year ahead of us at school or an older sister.

Why write a book at all at this stage of my career? One word: television. If I hadn't joined the cast of my father's reality show, *The Apprentice*, we wouldn't even be having this discussion. The show has been a huge hit, at one point drawing more than 50 million viewers each week. And it's changed just about everything for me. Despite my very public upbringing, I'd always been a very private person, and up until I joined the show I was able to go about my business and do my thing in a stealthy sort of way. I liked that. Nobody paid much attention to me beyond the transactions themselves. I was able to make my presence known around a conference table or on a construction site, but if we weren't dealing with each other directly you wouldn't have recognized me. I was a private person, working out of range of the public eye. Television changed all that, right away. I'm not even the star of the show, just a supporting player, but I started to get tons of mail from viewers, starting with my very first appearance. Reality television is such an intimate genre, people can't help but see you as you are—and they seemed to respond to me. Now that I was something of a celebrity, they appeared to like that I was cut a little differently than other successful young women of my generation, that I seemed more focused on building a career and making my family proud than on partying and hamming it up in front of the cameras. I heard from mothers, thanking me for setting such a positive example for their daughters. And I heard from those daughters, asking for advice on how to make it in the business world.

I thought that was pretty cool. Unexpected but pretty cool. And the more I thought about it, the more it made sense. After all, my brothers and I were the original "apprentices." We'd spent most of our lives learning the ins and outs of business from our parents. No, Donald Trump couldn't fire us—not until we started working for him, at least—but in every other respect it was a full-on apprenticeship.

Millions of people had turned to him for advice and inspiration over the years, so it was inevitable that a new generation of aspiring entrepreneurs would look to us for our own takes on the Trump formula. At first I tried to respond to as many of the letters and e-mails as I could—but ultimately that was impossible. So I approached the situation the same way I would have tackled any other dilemma: I came at it from a new angle. I thought, How can I reach out to all these young women in a more efficient way?

One more word to explain my inspiration to write a book. Actually, one name: Oprah. I'd been invited onto her show to promote my new jewelry line—my first solo venture outside our core family business. I was terrifically excited, because I'd always been a huge Oprah Winfrey fan. During our interview, she complimented me for managing to avoid the traps that ensnare many other children of privilege and for staying focused on making my own mark in the world. It was such an honor to hear her say that. But there was an even bigger thrill. She was wearing a stunning pair of my earrings—O-shaped, of course—from the Ivanka Trump Collection. I'd given them to Oprah as a thank-you gift for having me on the show, but I'd never expected her to wear them while I was on the set. It was such a gracious gesture, I thought.

A few days after the taping, I received a lovely handwritten letter from Oprah, thanking me for the earrings and congratulating me on my various accomplishments. She even called me a role model for the twenty-first-century woman. It was another gracious gesture, but it was more than the letter itself that touched me. It was what Oprah had to say. Her words meant so much that I had the letter framed and keep it on my office desk.

I hope Oprah won't mind that I'm sharing so much with you, because she's one of *my* role models. I think she's the most influential businesswoman in the world, so I took her words as a kind of charge— to share my own insights and experiences with anyone who cared to sign on for the ride. Therefore, a book: one that I hope can be a resource for young women starting their careers or perhaps looking to rejuvenate them, in today's incredibly challenging economic environment. And it's not just the business landscape that's so challenging for young women. It's our personal path, as well. There are so many choices out there for us, so many opportunities, so many twists and turns that we can hardly anticipate. It's all too easy to take one tiny misstep in the wrong direction and end up on a completely wrong road.

And so I set about it.

RUSSELL SIMMONS—Record producer, hip-hop mogul

ON GIVING

I talk to a lot to people who are in struggle, a lot of kids who don't have a lot of faith, and I try to get them to realize that they already have everything they need. Everybody is given everything they need, all the time. We know that because it's in every scripture. And the real truth is, when you're comfortable with what you have, you attract other things. Think of the most successful people you know. They go to work, they say they need to work, but they really don't need anything. *That's why* things *like* them. They attract success. It's basic: when you go to work from a place of abundance and you operate from a place where you already have everything, you work harder and smarter because your mind is clear and your focus is strong.

So I'm always telling young people to count their blessings. Start from a place of strength. Get up in the morning, and decide what you're going to give. All that taking stuff is secondary. It's giving. I mean, you've got to give to get, right? Good givers are great getters. That's the reason you're here. You need to become a great servant, first and foremost. Everything else will follow. And it's not as if we have to change the way we are. Most of the young people I work with, they wake up in the morning, they want to be servants. It's in us already. We want to give something back, put something out there. If you're a record producer, you come across a hot record, you start to think, Wait till they hear this! You're not thinking about the money you'll make, although the money will come. You're thinking, Wait until they hear this record! You're excited. You want to share it. If it's clothing, you're thinking, Wait till they try on this shirt! It's hot! Anything creative, it's like that. Any service.

In business, we should always be looking to give something that brings lasting happiness. Something we believe in. You want to be proud of your product, proud of what you're giving your customers. That's what will make your product or service stand out, because people can feel that. Your commitment to excellence, to strength, to purpose, it all shines through. That's where you find your success.

You don't trick the world, you feed the world.

ONE

FAMILY MATTERS

> Every great mistake has a halfway moment, a split second
> when it can be recalled and perhaps remedied.
>
> —PEARL S. BUCK

The opportunities I've been given are laden with accountability. I feel that deeply now as an adult—at times maybe a little *too* deeply—but it wasn't so long ago that I was a typical rebellious teenager, not really stopping to think how my actions reflected on my parents or the reputation we all shared. One casebook example stands out: I was fifteen years old, away at Choate, off on some grand adventure with my boarding school friends. One of us hit on the idea of getting our navels pierced, and the next thing we knew we were in a funky little jewelry shop, pooling our money to make sure we each had enough to cover the procedure.

Now I happen to cringe a little bit whenever I see a young girl sporting a belly button ring—but that's just what I was at the time, a young girl. A lot of my friends sport non-ear body pierces and that's great for them but not for me—yet I nearly took the plunge with my fifteen-year-old classmates. It's the quintessential harmless act of teenage rebellion, right? I don't remember ever wanting to pierce my navel before that one day, but there I was, caught up in the moment, going through the motions with my friends.

17

Luckily, I didn't go first. I was in the back room of the jewelry shop with a friend on the table. I was next and good to go. No doubt in my mind. No qualms. (Well . . . maybe *some* qualms, considering my friend's nervous yelps.) But then my cell phone rang. It was my father, calling to check in and see what I was up to.

They always had great timing, my parents. Somehow, throughout my childhood, they managed to thwart most of my bad or impulsive decisions before I could even make them. And it's not that I was a rotten kid. Quite the opposite; I was pretty good. I got good grades, worked hard, made mostly good choices. But like any teenager, I had my moments—and whenever I did, one of my parents would usually turn up. It's as if their antennae were set in just the right way. And just then my dad just happened to call with a real, in-my-face reminder that he would kick my butt if I got my belly button pierced. My mother, too. It was so unladylike, they'd say. So undignified. So unnecessary. And they would have been right. Again, nothing against my friends or anyone who's made a different choice with their own bodies. I respect that. But it wasn't for me. And it took hearing from my father at just that moment for me to remind myself of that.

It wasn't only my parents' disapproval that made me realize I was about to make a big mistake. And it's not as if I was *really* afraid of the consequences. I mean, what's a month-long grounding against the sweet swagger of a killer belly-button ring? But hearing from my dad at just that moment got me thinking about the responsibility I carried. Even as a boarding school brat out on the town, I recognized this. At least I started to, there in the back room of that jewelry shop. And it wasn't a responsibility to my parents, although that was certainly part of it. It was a responsibility to myself above all. To do the right thing. To carry myself with pride and confidence and dignity. To preserve and protect the family name and reputation—which, after all, were now my name and reputation, too. To leave myself open to every possibility, every opportunity, every advantage.

My father didn't know where I was, of course. He didn't know what I was planning. But I've often thought back on that moment in that jewelry shop as emblematic. It wasn't just that my parents had good instincts that kept me and my brothers honest and focused and headed down the right road. It wasn't that they had impeccable timing. It's that they were *always* there. Even when they weren't in the room with me, or in the same town, they were present. They called. They kept in constant touch. And when you're in constant touch, you don't have to worry about impeccable timing. You can't help but hit it right, just by being there. Sure, a part of me knows that I might be reading too much into this one moment. I mean, my father just happened to call. It was just a coincidence, right? But then another part of me gets that he just happened to call because he *always* just happened to call. Because without even knowing it, he'd stumbled onto yet another life lesson—something else he could give me to help me grow my game.

REMEMBER THE LEGOS

Of course, my parents couldn't always be present, just as I couldn't quite make it to a few of my own influential moments. Consider this one slightly out-of-focus childhood memory, and you'll get what I mean: for the longest time, I looked back on a long-ago Christmas when I'd gotten into some little-kid trouble for gluing together several pieces of my new LEGO set, which I'd gotten as a gift that year. I remembered it as one of the formative episodes of my growing up— and, in this way, I suppose it was. I could actually close my eyes and picture it. My idea, I recalled, had been to build a plastic, primary-colored skyscraper (my first construction project!) and then, once I'd gone to all that trouble, to preserve it for posterity. That explained the glue. I'd taken a brand-new toy and turned it into an art project, which meant that my brothers and I could never play with it again. That explained the punishment.

For years and years, the memory was close enough to touch. I grew up with it. I shared it with friends. I loved how it showed the way I'd leaned toward real estate at an early age, the way I'd defied convention by using those LEGO blocks in such an unconventional way, the way my father seemed to take pride in my precocious behavior even as he and my mother had to punish me for it, and on and on.

I happened to mention the story not too long ago to my brothers, and they looked at me as if I'd sprouted horns. They couldn't believe I was claiming ownership of "the LEGO incident." According to my brothers, *they* were the ones who had built the skyscraper and glued the pieces together. *They* were the ones who'd gotten punished. *They* were the ones who looked back on this moment as one of the first manifestations of my father's influence. *They'd* told it to their friends over the years, too.

I thought, Hmmm, that's interesting. Not at all the way I'd filed it away in my head—but I wasn't prepared to buy my brothers' version just yet. You have to realize, in our family you sometimes had to fight to make your point or to stake your claim to an idea, so I went to the most reliable arbiter I could think of to settle the matter: my father. The next time we were all together, one of us brought it up. I was so firm in my view that this was *my* anecdote, *my* sign of big things to come, that I didn't really need my father's validation on this. I needed it only to shut my brothers up. I knew the real story. After all, I was there. It was Don and Eric who had an issue.

But then my father weighed in with his own take—and upended the entire memory. "Sorry, kids," he said, "but you're all wrong. That's actually *my* story. That was me and your uncle Robert. Only it wasn't LEGOs, I'm afraid. Just old-fashioned wooden building blocks. I don't think we even had LEGOs when I was a kid. But we took these wooden blocks and built this wonderful building and glued all the pieces together so it wouldn't fall down."

He went on to explain that he'd even written about the incident in his first book, *The Art of the Deal,* which must have been where I'd gotten the story in the first place. My brothers, too. We'd all read Dad's books as soon as we were old enough, and we must each have found a point of connection in this one tossed-off story, to where we somehow filed it away and made it our own. Subconsciously. Instinctively. So it's not the story itself that rates a mention; it's not the gluing together of blocks to preserve and protect one of the first-ever Trump towers. It's not even the tug and pull over our family legacies that I find so interesting. It's the way my brothers and I seemed to grab at this memory as emblematic. The way we each came to own it, throughout our childhoods and well into our own first steps as young professionals, working at our father's side building actual skyscrapers. The way it reinforces how the fuzzy, uncertain eye of memory can sometimes take us to a deeper, more fundamental understanding of how things really were than the plain, unvarnished truth might tell us in the first place.

Mostly, though, the story stands as one of the first and best examples of how we work together as a family. It's very much a collaborative effort, so much so that none of us can claim ownership of any single idea or initiative. We bounce everything off one another in such a way that each of us is able to own the projects we're working on. In my father's book, the LEGO story was just a cute and possibly revealing childhood memory, but in mine I set it out in the hope that it will reveal something more: how we were as a family, how we kids tried to be like our father—and, ultimately, how we relied on one another.

In real estate, you need a strong foundation if you hope to build a solid structure. That's no metaphor; it's Construction 101. The same holds if you mean to build a strong career in business. It needs to happen on a real foundation. Again, this is no metaphor; it's business. And it's basic. For me that's the great and abiding takeaway from this shared memory. That character begins at home. We take it in by example, early on and ever after. Even as adults, we draw from mentors and role models to help give purpose and focus to our lives and our work, but it's the influences of our childhood that resonate most of all—even if they take the form of an "adopted" memory my brothers and I had somehow lifted from my father's autobiography and had come to regard as our own.

GROWING UP TRUMP

I had an interesting childhood, I'll say that. I grew up in a kind of fishbowl, and it had my father's name on it. Granted, it was my name too, but it felt mostly like his, up there in big, bold letters on the sides of our buildings. Our *homes*.

That said, I really didn't give it much thought, seeing our name displayed on the sides of our buildings like that, until I went away to boarding school. The dorms at Choate were the first buildings I lived in that didn't say "Trump" somewhere on the facade, and I remember thinking that this was worth noting. (Only to myself, of course—until now.) I looked around at all the bright, impressive students—children of privilege, mostly, but also children of all backgrounds who felt truly lucky to be able to attend one of the most prestigious boarding schools on the planet—and I realized this wasn't exactly a common dilemma. It wasn't a big deal, either, but it struck me as symbolic, considering the path I would carve for myself from there on out. Even at fourteen and fifteen years old, I had something of an independent streak, I guess. I loved my parents, I loved my family, I loved the opportunities their hard work and success provided for me and my brothers—but I was determined to branch out on my own. To look at the world from a whole new angle.

Even if it meant living in a building named for someone else!

Let's get back to that fishbowl for a moment—because in some respects, to some people, it's as if I never left. I get that. When you grow up in the public eye, as I did, people tend to see you a certain way—for a long, long time. I get that, too. My father enjoyed some of his first prominent successes during the 1980s, and he and my mother generated a ton of publicity as a couple. In addition to my father's accomplishments in real estate and in his other businesses, my parents were also very involved in the New York social circle, particularly on the charity circuit. This was primarily my mother's scene, but my father attended his share of business dinners and industry events. They were always out and about, racing to some event or other, to the point where our comings and goings were inevitably and unavoidably the target of media attention. All of this seemed perfectly normal to me at the time, but it meant that from the very beginning, people came to know me as a kind of princess, surrounded by toys and trips and trinkets that most little girls could only dream of.

Yet even though the material aspects of my childhood appear to stand out, the most important and enduring gifts I received from my parents were their values: self-sufficiency, hard work, respect. To others on the outside looking in, it might seem that our family symbolized a whole different set of values or that our lifestyle was fairly synonymous with the glitz, glamour, and greed of the 1980s. But that wasn't my experience. Not at all. We were surrounded by fine things. We traveled the world and enjoyed a kind of front-row seat before the world stage. The Trump name came to mark my father's signature style: big, bold, luxurious, and daring. But my parents made sure that their children were grounded and principled and that we knew these privileges and our big, bold advantages came as the result of their dedication and determination and that they were never to be taken for granted.

It went back to how they were raised.

My mother, Ivana Zelniček, was born in the small Czechoslovakian town of Gottwaldov, just south of Prague in what is now known as the Czech Republic. My grandfather Milós—"Dedo" to family and friends—was an electrical engineer who helped design many of the sports stadiums in Czechoslovakia. My grandmother Maria—"Babi"—was a homemaker with a passion for reading and cooking.

In addition to his many and varied accomplishments in engineering, my maternal grandfather was an excellent skier who taught my mother to ski when she was only two years old. She showed a real talent for it and managed to win her first race by the age of six. She would go on to win many more competitions, eventually earning a spot on Czechoslovakia's ski team in the 1968 Olympics. My mother's success as a skier had a major impact on her life—and on mine, too, as it turned out. As a world-class athlete, she had access to better food, better clothing, and better housing than other Czech citizens, so even though she grew up in a Communist country, she did so with every material advantage available in that Spartan context—all of it earned. On a personal level, her rigorous training schedule helped to develop and strengthen the tireless work ethic she would carry with her into adulthood and into her new life in the United States. And it nourished a fiercely competitive streak that would become one of her defining characteristics.

The most significant fringe benefit of my mother's athletic prowess was the freedom it afforded her for international travel—and she took full advantage of it. Without the special privileges given to athletes, she would have never made her way to North America and eventually to the United States. After graduating from Prague's Charles University in 1972, she took a trip to Canada to pursue the modeling career she'd begun in Prague. A lot of people think my father was the one with the dogged determination and discipline to succeed—but my mother was racing, modeling, and studying, all in a high-level way. Once in Canada, she fell in love with a Czech émigré named George Syrovatka who was working as a ski instructor. The relationship lasted only a few years, but when it was over my mother was in no hurry to return to her life behind the Iron Curtain. So she stayed on in Canada, and when her days as a competitive skier came to an end she turned her attention more fully to modeling, another meaningful turn.

Even as a young woman, my mother knew what she wanted. When she set her mind to something, she usually succeeded. She signed with a prestigious modeling agency and in 1976 was selected as one of several Canadian models to travel to New York on a tour to promote the upcoming Summer Olympic Games, to be held in Montreal. One night in New York during her extended visit, my mother and a few of her model friends went to dinner at a restaurant called Maxwell's Plum, a well-known hot spot at the time. In fact, it was so popular they couldn't get a table. At first.

As they were about to leave in frustration, my father happened to notice them. Donald Trump was a successful young real estate developer with an old-fashioned sense of chivalry. He was sitting with a large group at a large table, so he asked my mother and her friends if they would like to join them. There was plenty of room, he said.

I heard this story all the time when I was a kid. My parents told it into the ground, and I always thought there was something quaint and old-fashioned about it, the way my father and his friends were so quick to make room at their table for my mother and her friends. It was the kind of chance, storybook meeting that seemed to belong in a fairy tale—and even though the story didn't turn out so wonderfully in the end (after all, my parents divorced), it did produce a happy ending. Or three: me and my two brothers.

BUILDING FROM THE GROUND UP

My father was born in Queens, New York, to Fred and Mary Trump. My paternal grandfather was the son of German immigrants. He met my grandmother while she was in America on a vacation from her native Scotland. They married in 1936 and settled in Queens, where my grandfather had started a business building single-family houses. Actually, he started out building garages as attachments to existing homes, as more and more families started to own cars. After World War II, as thousands of soldiers returned to New York looking for housing, my grandfather's business started to take off, and before long he was one of the biggest builders of middle-class housing in Brooklyn, Queens, and Staten Island. He saw an opportunity and rose to meet it—a thread that runs through our family quilt in an intricate way.

My father was a real handful growing up. He never really went into great detail with us on this, except to say that he didn't always make the best choices and couldn't quite seem to steer clear of trouble. At thirteen, my grandparents sent him to a military school north of New York City, hoping the strict structure would help focus some of his energy and drive. The plan worked: my father thrived as a cadet, captaining the baseball team, earning academic honors, and even leading the school's contingent down Fifth Avenue in the 1963 Columbus Day Parade—past the future site of Trump Tower. After graduating from military school, my father enrolled at Fordham University in the Bronx, thinking he would keep a hand in the family real estate business while he pursued his degree. After two years, he transferred to the Wharton School of Finance at the University of Pennsylvania, believing he would benefit from a more challenging academic environment—a path my brother Don and I would later follow.

One of the great themes of my father's life and career has been his ability to think big. If something was working in a modest way he'd look to make it work in a bigger way. "Modest" wasn't part of his vocabulary. When he graduated from Wharton and started working with my grandfather, who was by then a thriving developer in New York's outer boroughs, my father's first thought was to kick things up another level. In his mind, the magic and the money of New York City lay in Manhattan, so he set his sights there. He bought an apartment on the Upper East Side and started spending most of his free time scouring the city, usually on foot, searching for the right property to allow the Trumps to break into the Manhattan market.

My father's first big idea for the family real estate business took root in the late 1970s, when New York was in a deepening financial crisis. The city itself was in debt, unemployment was up, crime was rampant, interest rates were rising, and many businesses were leaving town. But where others saw upheaval and uncertainty, my father saw opportunity, signaling another great theme of his career: the ability to turn left while all around him people were turning right. One of the strategies he'd learned from his father was to defy conventional wisdom—or at least to consider alternatives. It's an approach I try to bring to every potential deal, to every new market, because if your instinct is to zig while everyone else is looking to zag, you're more likely to discover an important new angle. An angle of opportunity. My father's conviction was that New York City would weather this financial crisis and that Manhattan would once again emerge as the greatest place to live in the world. Rather than flee the city, my father was determined to invest—heavily!—while the terms were favorable.

He finally found the property he was looking for: the old Commodore Hotel above Grand Central Station. Looking back, it's no wonder my father targeted this particular asset. Over the years, he's been drawn to landmark buildings in landmark locations. His thinking was always that, if they were positioned correctly, there were certain value-added elements to these iconic sites, and with this deal he would have his first chance to put his thinking into play. There was a lot to like about this deal, he told us later, when we were old enough to understand his logic: Grand Central Station was one of the city's transportation hubs, but by the middle 1970s it too was struggling. The station was in serious need of a face-lift, and the once-proud and stately Commodore could have benefited from one, too. The surrounding neighborhood wasn't in such great shape, either. My father knew full well that without a complete refurbishment to attract new customers, the hotel would drift deeper into disrepair and soon go out of business, but he also knew there weren't too many developers with the guts, the temperament, or the deep pockets to pursue a deal to revitalize the property in the middle of such an economic downturn.

For the first time in his career, my father used uncertainty to advantage. He had the guts and temperament to make it work, but he couldn't exactly afford it. He knew he could buy the hotel at a very low price, but he needed a sweetener for the deal to fully make sense. He correctly suspected that the city would not want to see its image further tarnished by having a dilapidated hotel adjacent to a main point of entry into Manhattan, so he used the specter of that negative image as leverage and negotiated a forty-year tax abatement with the city. The terms were so favorable that his competitors and critics were stunned—and probably a little incensed. It was such an unprecedented deal that most developers wouldn't even have thought to ask for it, but my father put the proposed abatement on the table because he had nothing to lose by doing so. The worst that could happen, he told me later, was that the city would turn him down and he would move on in search of another property. Or they would negotiate.

As a direct result of the acquisition of the Commodore, which he reopened as the Grand Hyatt, my father became the poster boy for a new breed of Manhattan real estate developer. It put him on the map and laid the foundation for the next phase of his career, allowing him to form his own company.

The lessons of that deal continue to resonate. As I write this, the city is once again on shaky ground. Unemployment is skyrocketing, city services are being slashed, the credit markets are tight, and businesses are being closed at an alarming rate. It feels like the dark days of the 1970s all over again, but just as my father was able to see past the doom and gloom and unearth a chance-of-a-lifetime deal that would catapult him to success, I know there are opportunities out there—even now (especially now), in this down market. I know that if I can be as diligent and tenacious as my father was when he was just starting out, if I can get creative and think against the grain, I can make a whole lot of noise.

ARIANNA HUFFINGTON—Cofounder and editor in chief, The Huffington Post

ON EMPOWERMENT

In order to conquer the workplace as women, we need to approach it in our own unique way, not as carbon copies of men—briefcase-carrying, pinstripe-wearing career machines who just happen to have vaginas. We're faced with a double challenge, because aside from the office and career anxieties everyone faces, women have specific work-related fears that center on the paradox of maintaining relationships and remaining "feminine" while still doing a good job. These are the fears of ambition and assertiveness.

We have to let go of the idea that we must be sweet all the time if we're going to be "real women." And we must learn not to internalize personal attacks. Let's face it, our culture still isn't comfortable with outspoken women. As Marlo Thomas put it, "A man has to be Joe McCarthy to be called ruthless. All a woman has to do is put you on hold." The best way to neutralize this kind of attitude is through laughing at it. The key is not to give others the power—and that includes the "obnoxious roommate" living in our head, constantly judging how we look, what we do, and what we say. Because in the end, there is nothing more important than not giving in to the fears and judgments we drain our spirits with.

It's also crucial for women to be really supportive of one another. We should build "fearlessness tribes" by surrounding ourselves with women—and men, of course—who will always be in our corner, always there for us, whether we succeed or fail. It's very important for older women, those who have gone before, to give a hand up to and to mentor their younger colleagues.

TWO

FINDING THE ANGLES OF OPPORTUNITY

Always bear in mind that your own resolution to succeed is
more important than any one thing.

—ABRAHAM LINCOLN

My parents hit it off that night at Maxwell's Plum—a chance encounter that would pay great dividends. They were married early in 1977. My brother Don was born later that year. I arrived in 1981, followed by my younger brother, Eric, two years later. Home was our apartment in Trump Tower, my father's signature building. By now, it's a well-known landmark, not only to New Yorkers but to fans of *The Apprentice* and millions of tourists who visit every year. My father finished the building not long after I was born, and we moved in as soon as our triplex apartment was ready. My bedroom was on the sixty-eighth floor. In many ways, it was a lot like the bedrooms of other little girls my age. I had a Madonna clock next to my white canopy bed. My walls were painted lilac and checkered with *90210* stickers and *Melrose Place* trading cards. (Luke Perry was my absolute favorite!) Plus the usual assortment of Bon Jovi, Mötley Crüe, and Paula Abdul posters hung around the room. I was a sucker for all those big-hair artists of the late 1980s and early 1990s.

In many more ways, though, you'd have to look long and hard to find another child's bedroom quite like it. There weren't too many girls growing up in Manhattan who had such an amazing view right outside their window. As a kid, I didn't really appreciate what that view might have been worth, on the high-flying end of the New York real estate market. But to me it was priceless. I loved waking up every morning and looking out on Central Park and at all the incredible buildings along its edges. I'm sure I took that view for granted, but it instilled in me from the very beginning an appreciation for construction and real estate and the sweep and grandeur of the city skyline.

SETTING THE TONE

As a future real estate developer, I suppose it also reinforced the notion that even my wildest dreams were within reach. Close enough to touch. Right outside my bedroom window. From there the skyline didn't seem as imposing as it did from the street. I came to know every building by name: the San Remo, the Majestic, the El Dorado, the Dakota . . . I learned their histories, as well, including which buildings were being renovated or sold or changed in any way. I knew who lived where—and, when I was a bit older, how much they'd paid for the privilege. Knowing the personalities inside each of these iconic buildings seemed to give each tower its own personality. This one was all high and mighty; that one, stately and dignified; and that other one, a little artsy and out there. I came to recognize and appreciate the different styles of architecture, the quality of the workmanship, the attention to detail that had gone into the construction and subsequent maintenance of these glorious structures. On a clear day, I could see past the mansions of Fifth Avenue's "Millionaires' Row" all the way north to Yankee Stadium—and beyond! All those magnificent buildings looked like little toys to me, playthings that I could move around or break down or reimagine, many of them inhabited by people I knew, or who had been to our house for dinner. It made the far-off notion of building something grand seem very possible, very real.

As I said, totally within reach.

I imagine my father came to regard the New York City skyline in much the same way, looking out from his own bedroom window or down from his Trump Tower office, which also faced the park. We never really talked about it in just this way, but when you soak in this kind of scenery on a daily basis it can't help but become a part of you. It makes the city itself seem less intimidating—and your goals appear just a little more attainable. Mostly it leaves you thinking anything is possible, and here I've bumped into one of the most sustaining lessons of my childhood—namely, that if you can envision something you can make it happen. In Donald and Ivana Trump, I was blessed with two of the best parents in the world—and the blessing ran not only to their warmth and love and parenting styles but to their impressive accomplishments. My brothers and I had some world-class role models. Our parents seemed to embody every template for our future success, every ground rule, everything we wanted to build for ourselves. Most of all, they seemed to enjoy reaching for the stars. As kids, all we had to do was watch them living out their dreams, filling their days with purpose and accomplishment, and know that when it was our time we could will it for ourselves.

Another sustaining lesson: hard work is everything. (Just to be clear, *will* can never replace *hard work*, but it's a necessary spark.) Sure, it was nice to grow up in such spectacular surroundings, with every conceivable luxury, but there were times when I would have traded all of that to have my parents around a little bit more. A lot of kids feel that way. But then I grew up a bit and realized how important work was to my father. How essential. Not just the finished product, or the payday that came his way as a result, but the work itself. He put in incredibly long hours building his empire and developing his public persona. Remember, he was a fairly young man when he made that big splash at Grand Central Station with his Commodore deal—still very much a work in progress. In time we would all come to know and appreciate how relentlessly and endlessly hard my father worked. When I was little, I remember him spending more than fifteen hours a day at the office on weekdays, and he'd log considerable time over the weekend as well. I used to think he drew great strength and nourishment from his work. It made him rich in more ways than one.

My mother worked constantly, too. She didn't seem to live to work, the way my father did, but she certainly loved it. For a time, she managed the Trump Castle Casino in Atlantic City and subsequently turned her attention to The Plaza Hotel in midtown Manhattan. With so many projects on their plates, my parents were pulled in many different directions. Yet even with all these demands on their time, they were always available to me and my brothers. Maybe not in the most typical ways, but in what ways they could be.

Here's one: I used to follow my mother around while she worked, and that became our special time together. After my father bought The Plaza, he put my mother in charge of the renovation and ultimately the management of the hotel. On many mornings, she'd bring me along, and for me it was like being taken to the world's most magical playground. I'd watch as she checked to make sure that a hallway was perfectly vacuumed, that the brass railings on the grand staircase had been polished, that the flowers in the lobby were fresh—even that the bellhops' uniforms were properly ironed.

Her attention to detail was legendary. When I was around eight years old, I remember walking through the lobby of the Trump Castle Casino with my mother and the general manager. The lobby was dominated by a massive chandelier, which seemed to swallow up the entire ceiling. It must have contained tens of thousands of lightbulbs. As we walked, the general manager brought my mother up to date on various items, but then she suddenly stopped him, pointing to the ceiling. "A lightbulb has blown," she announced. It was the most astonishing thing. I hadn't even noticed her looking up, but an alarm must have gone off in the back of her head, and she pointed it out and made sure it was taken care of.

My mother was something of a marvel at our Trump properties. Recently, I was on a walk-through of our Trump SoHo construction site when I struck up a conversation with one of the ironworkers. He told me a story about my mother that he'd actually heard from his father, who had worked on the Commodore renovation all those years ago. (As you can see, the Trump Organization is truly a family business—over the years, we've employed several generations of several different families.) Before reopening the Commodore as the Grand Hyatt, my father put my mother in charge of overseeing the interior design, even though she was pregnant with my older brother at the time.

True to form, my mother was relentless, focusing on every last detail. According to my second-generation ironworker source, she'd start "busting balls," the moment she turned up at the site every morning. (He said this with great admiration and respect for my mother, by the way—and not just because I was her daughter! She *really* made an impression!) Nothing escaped her attention: she'd tell one worker to move a crown molding a quarter of an inch, another to replace a light switch because it was ever so slightly crooked. She was unwilling to compromise on the small imperfections that most people don't even notice. As a result, the workers would be quaking in their Timberlands at the sight of my mother, knowing that she was going to hound them about some seemingly insignificant detail or other. When she finally entered the last weeks of her pregnancy, they were all extremely excited—for my parents, of course, but also for the reprieve my mother's looming maternity leave seemed to offer the guys on the crew.

On New Year's Eve 1977, my mother made one final inspection of the site, then went home and gave birth to Donny later that night. Two days later, on January 2, the workers returned to the job site, looking forward to at least a few weeks away from my mother's demanding presence. They were just a couple of hours into their shift when my mother showed up—back on the job, back on their cases, after a maternity leave of less than forty-eight hours!

So much for their hoped-for reprieve.

Her unwavering commitment to excellence, all the way down to the smallest detail, made a real impression on me. To this day, when I visit our hotel properties around the world, I feel as if I'm channeling my mother from back in her Plaza days. In fact, when my brothers and I wrote the Trump Organization's first formal "Brand Standard Manual," one of our goals was to make sure we continued to meet and surpass the quality standards my mother had put in place at The Plaza and the other properties she oversaw—all the way down to the smallest details.

MAKING TIME

Oh, how I loved going to The Plaza with my mother when I was a little girl! Once she made her rounds, I was allowed to go off and play, and I'd spend hours running through the endless hallways, riding the elevators, snooping around the basement, and exploring all the nooks and crannies of the historic hotel. The workers there used to joke that I was the real-life Eloise—and I guess I was. The Eloise from the classic children's books by Kay Thompson lived on the top floor of The Plaza with her nanny, her dog, and her pet turtle. I got to go home at night, and my pet turtles never seemed to survive much longer than a month or two, but in every other respect I really did feel like Eloise, and I came to cherish those visits to the hotel, not just for the grand adventures that lay in wait but also for the chance to be with my mother and watch her go about her business.

My father made time for me at work, too. He'd stop whatever he was doing, at least for a few precious moments, whenever I called. Even if he was in the middle of an important meeting or call, he'd make me feel as if he had all the time in the world for me. And it wasn't just an act; he really did make the time. Years later, I learned that he had actually been putting me on the speakerphone if someone happened to be in his office. Politicians, athletes, union leaders, bankers, visiting dignitaries of one stripe or another—it didn't matter to my father. These important people would just have to wait while he helped his little girl sort through whatever it was that needed sorting through or while he took the time to ask how my day was at school or how I'd done on a particular test. I can't imagine those VIP types were too happy about being kept waiting, but my father didn't seem to mind. I always thought that was so great, the way he'd set aside whatever he was doing to make time for me. Nothing was more important.

At least that's how I was always made to feel, just as I was with my mother, who was also always on the go. My mother is an exuberant woman, filled with a passion for life and adventure that made it hard for her to stay in one place for long. Even today, when she can certainly pull back and move about at a more leisurely pace, she likes nothing more than to get out in the world and take on a new challenge. My parents are strikingly similar in that regard. They've grown apart, and even when they were together they seemed to be cut in different ways, but they do share an approach to life: all out, all the time. Both are incredibly ambitious, driven, competitive, confident, straightforward, loyal people. Both have an astonishingly large appetite for life. Neither one of them fit into any kind of traditional parenting role when I was a kid, and I can't imagine either one of them being content to be at home for dinner every night at six o'clock or to spend their weekends going to soccer games or ballet recitals. It just wasn't their thing—and I understood and appreciated that about them at an early age.

It's not as though my brothers and I were shortchanged by my parents' occasional absences. They made sure there was a tremendous support system in place at home, so that we kids got the love and attention we needed, even if it didn't always come directly from them. In fact, outside my parents, I'd have to say my biggest childhood influences were Bridget and Dorothy, the two wonderful Irish nannies who looked after us. And my maternal grandparents, Babi and Dedo, were around to help fill in the gaps. My grandparents had a system: they'd come to New York and live with us for two months, then return to the Czech Republic for two months. I really loved it when they visited. Babi was a hands-on grandmother, straight out of Central Casting. She helped to cultivate my interests in reading and cooking. There was always the strong smell of Eastern European cooking wafting from our kitchen whenever Babi was in town.

Dedo was a true outdoorsman, and it's because of him that my brothers learned to hunt and fish and hike. If it had been up to my father, they would have been out on the golf course or playing tennis, but they really took to Dedo's pursuits.

Me, I was content to hang back in the kitchen with my grandmother. (I didn't learn to cook until I was much older—but back then I certainly ate!) Or I'd follow along in my mother's wake as she made her rounds at The Plaza. We all loved that great hotel, my father most of all. When he purchased The Plaza in 1988, he called it "the Mona Lisa of Manhattan architecture." He even went on record saying that it was the only building he'd ever purchased simply because it was an architectural masterpiece and a true New York City landmark. Of course, it didn't hurt that it was also a good investment, but he wasn't ashamed to admit that he felt a visceral connection to the property.

Here again, I saw my father take yet another angle of opportunity— this one through the heart. He built on his emotional attachment to a piece of property and found a way to make it work from a business perspective as well.

MARKET MATTERS

The entrepreneurial spirit was very much alive among us Trump kids, but time and circumstance invariably conspired against us. During the first season of *The Apprentice*, my father suggested to the show's producer, Mark Burnett, that they develop a project to help determine the most basic business instincts of the contestants—namely, to start a lemonade stand on the streets of New York and see who could earn the most money from sales. What could be more basic than that? It was a classic test of street smarts, business acumen, and shift-on-the-fly ingenuity, and it ended up being one of the most popular and memorable segments of the show. My brothers and I used to gather around and watch some of those first-season shows together, and I remember thinking what a shame it was that we never really had the same opportunity as little kids to show our parents what we could do.

Trump Lemonade? With a name like that, we couldn't help but clean up, right? But we never got the chance.

The best thing about a lemonade stand, from a little-kid perspective, is that it's a no-lose proposition. Most kids I knew had their parents supply the lemonade, the cups, the ice. The barriers to entry were next to nothing. Some parents even helped scout out a prime location. We had no such advantages. First of all, my mother wasn't about to let us set up shop with a lemonade stand at Fifth Avenue and 57th Street— and to do so in the lobby of Trump Tower would have been just a little too precious, don't you think? And we certainly couldn't go selling our product door-to-door to our well-heeled neighbors. This was one of the few times—I was about six years old—when the larger-than-life aspects of our childhood seemed to collide with some of the more mundane, smaller-than-life rites of passage other kids got to enjoy. Still, we kept pressing the matter, and we finally set up our first lemonade stand during one summer at our house in Greenwich, Connecticut—only it fell to us kids to supply our own inventory. Sort of. We didn't actually go out and buy the lemonade, but we did have to keep track of the costs and agree to reimburse "the house" out of our first proceeds.

The only trouble with this arrangement was our location—not a typical Trump problem. We were at the end of a cul-de-sac in an affluent community of spacious homes on sprawling properties. In every other respect, this was a prime spot, but it was a dead zone for aspiring lemonade magnates. We could see only one other house, which basically meant there was no traffic. No cars. No pedestrians. No stray dogs, even. We were doomed, until our wily charms and persuasive marketing skills somehow managed to save the day—at least enough to cover our expenses. As good fortune would have it, we had a bodyguard that summer, and it fell to him to watch us in an unobtrusive way whenever we left our front yard. That cast him as our target market, and by the end of the afternoon we got this poor guy to drink so much lemonade it's a wonder his bladder didn't burst. Just to keep us in business. I think we also sold a fair amount to my parents' driver, as he came and went, and to some of the household staff, who took pity on us and dug deep for their spare change.

We made the best of a bad situation, I guess—a lesson we'd utilize again and again as we moved on in business.

Our next business venture was a bit more successful, but it was built on a dubious foundation. First, some setup is needed. I was a bit of a tomboy, which played into one of our most successful money-making schemes; you wouldn't have guessed it by looking at me, because my mother used to dress me in frills and lace and all the latest fashions, but underneath I had a pretty rambunctious spirit. There was definitely some duality to my persona, despite my perfect little-lady appearance. For a long while, I was obsessed with "boy toys" such as Tonka trucks, erector sets, and LEGOs.

Basically, if it had anything at all to do with digging or building, I was all over it. I loved crawling around in the dirt, moving all that earth with my miniature dump trucks, and pretending I was preparing some big tract of land for my father. It wasn't until I was eight or nine years old that I realized all my little girlfriends were busy playing with Barbie dolls, so I made an effort to change things and fall into line. This lasted about a week. I changed Barbie's outfits a couple of times and played with her accessories, and then I was done. It seemed so boring to me. I couldn't see the point. I didn't mind dressing up myself, trying on my mother's jewelry, or pretending to be a runway model, but I couldn't understand spending all that time and energy on a bunch of plastic dolls, so I put all my Barbies in a closet and forgot about them. For all I know, they're still there.

It was time well spent, though, because it taught me a valuable lesson: just because the other girls enjoyed something didn't mean I had to, too. I could still dress like a girl, act like a girl, and certainly look like a girl, but I had to be true to what actually interested me, not to what was *supposed* to interest me. I was never going to be happy living up to someone else's expectations. I would be sugar-and-spice-and-all-things-nice *and* snakes-and-snails-and-puppy-dog-tails, all at once.

So I fell into line alongside my brothers, with our trucks and our Matchbox cars and our digging tools. We were constantly chasing one another through the woods in the back of our property, playing cowboys and Indians, and pretending to shoot bows and arrows. Our adventures led us directly to our first real moneymaking scheme, and I'm afraid the emphasis was on *scheme,* because there was no real business—only the appearance of one. One of us hit on the idea of carving fake Native American artifacts from the rocks and stones we'd find in the woods. We'd chip away at them until they looked somewhat authentic, like actual ancient arrowheads, and then bury them in strategic spots so that we could come across them while we were running around with our friends. At that point, we'd turn around and sell them for a nice profit—around five dollars or so, depending on the piece and what we thought the market would bear. Once we came across these "finds" a time or two, we were able to do away with the charade of digging them up and focus on the manufacturing end.

VALUE THE CUSTOMER

I'm ashamed to admit it, but we did fairly well. To this day, I'll visit an old friend and learn that he or she still has one of our fake arrowheads among his or her prized childhood possessions. Our friends still believe some Native American shot that arrow in the wilds of Greenwich, Connecticut, hundreds of years ago. I can't imagine my father would be terribly proud of us for taking advantage of our neighborhood pals this way. His big thing, in every transaction, was to structure a sale in such a way that each side could benefit. The whole win-win concept was very important to him, even though he liked it when he could win a little bit more than the person across the negotiating table. Still, he liked to impart real value in a transaction, to give other people what they wanted, especially when selling real estate, and he did just that. In fact, he consistently *overdelivered* on his promises, and that quickly helped build the value of our brand and became one of the main reasons why our buyers are incredibly loyal and look to purchase in more than one Trump building. Our neighborhood friends from Greenwich, on the other hand, aren't exactly seeking me out to buy any more arrowheads.

There was one time, though, when my father couldn't overdeliver in his usual way. In fact, for reasons entirely out of his control, he underdelivered in a big way. The back-story: Before running The Plaza, my mother had been in charge of the Trump Castle Casino in Atlantic City, another amazing place for us kids to visit. It was always a treat when the casino security guards would take us into a kids' playroom, filled with old-school video and arcade games. The guards would give each of us a giant cup filled with quarters, thus ensuring that we would be amused for hours. I could never quite manage the mechanical-arm machine, where you attempt to grab a toy or stuffed animal from a glass case with a claw you manipulate from a control panel. I still see those machines in chain restaurants and arcades, and I always steer clear, because I never beat one of them legitimately. (Now, of course, I realize that a lot of arcade games are rigged—in this case, to have limp claws.) Even with a cupful of quarters, I could never snag a prize. Fortunately, this was one of those situations where being the daughter of Donald and Ivana Trump came in pretty handy, because when I ran out of money and started to look good and frustrated, a security guard would wander over, unlock the glass case, and hand me the stuffed animal of my choice.

Sucked being me, huh?

My favorite part about hanging out in Atlantic City was going to boxing matches with my parents. It was the tomboy in me. For a time in the late 1980s it seemed as if a great fight took place every weekend. I loved walking into the arena with my brothers and my parents and seeing all the colorful personalities milling about—politicians, movie stars, hustlers, sports heroes, and high rollers from Japan and Saudi Arabia. Then as now, boxing attracted an eclectic crowd. It was a little overwhelming to me as a child, but I remember taking enormous pride in the fact that my parents were so relaxed and in such complete control, even in that wild environment. I'd watch my father work the room, shaking hands with all those incredible characters, while my mother would hold court by our ringside seats, usually decked out in a rhinestone mini or a large-shouldered cocktail number. Then the fight would start, and we'd settle in to watch legendary boxers such as Mike Tyson, Evander Holyfield, and Sugar Ray Leonard decimate their opponents.

My brothers and I were usually the only kids in the arena—another one of the perks of having your name on the marquee out front—and we'd get flecked by blood and sweat when one of the fighters took a hard hit to the jaw. I just sat there in my sweet little dress with my sweet little bow in my hair, yelling my sweet little head off.

On this night, a young Mike Tyson was facing the not-so-young Michael Spinks in a title bout. Spinks had been the heavyweight champion and had never lost his title in the ring, but due to inactivity and other controversies he was no longer recognized by the boxing authorities as the world title holder. Tyson was the sport's latest sensation. I was just seven years old, but even I got swept up in all the excitement. My father was especially excited, because it was such a huge sporting event for Atlantic City. People flew in from all over the world to watch the fight, expecting a long, grueling bout. But then Tyson knocked out Spinks in just ninety-one seconds, and the place went crazy. Not in a good way. It felt for a few tense moments as if a riot were about to break out. All those high rollers had spent thousands and thousands of dollars to see a championship bout, and all they got to see was one punch. They were livid. People started yelling that the fight was fixed and demanding their money back.

At one point, my father hopped into the ring to quiet the crowd. He was dressed impeccably in a classic power suit—a real eighties look. I remember thinking he was so brave, so confident, so charismatic, trying to take control like that. I was just a little girl, but I was awestruck. I imagine it was a scary scene, but it never occurred to me to feel afraid because my father was there, taking charge and doing his best to give the audience what they wanted.

I've always remembered that moment. My father remembered it, too. Years later, he told me he'd felt terrible about that fight, because all those people were acting as if they'd been cheated. Not the high rollers, who could certainly take the hit, but the hardworking, blue-collar types, who'd driven down from New York or up from Philadelphia and had looked forward to the fight for weeks. There was nothing my father could have done; that's just how the fight played out in the ring. But he felt for all those people. They were buying into the glitz and glamour of the event as much as they were paying to see the fight itself, but he would have liked to have given them a better show, and for some reason I think back on that moment and our devious behavior with those fake arrowheads. We made a couple of bucks, but we should have known better. We'd duped our little friends and sold a lie, and it was harmless enough. But it took picturing my father in his snappy suit, quieting that angry Atlantic City fight crowd, for me to realize the importance of honesty and integrity in every business deal. In my father's view, this runs to your relationships and partnerships as well. Whenever possible, you want your client or customer or associate to feel good about the transaction, and that time it appeared that his high-roller casino guests would be going home disappointed. Even though there was nothing my father could have done about it, he was out there trying to make things right, in what ways he could.

That electric night in Atlantic City made me realize that it isn't enough to win a transaction. You have to be able to look the other guy in the eye and know that there is value in the deal on the other end, too—unless, of course, you're a onetime seller and just going for the gold.

I was just a kid, though, and still had a lot to learn. And if I paid attention to the positive example of my parents, I just might pick up a thing or two.

ROGER AILES—President, FOX News Channel

ON BEING POSITIVE

The single most important thing you can do in business is stay away from negative people. They're like building a quicksand pit for yourself. That's one of the common traits I see in successful people. Everything's always great and getting better—even when it isn't. That kind of positive approach is important, because if you listen to negative people you'll get a migraine. You'll never get anywhere. Some people turn whining into a career, but those people can be so depressing. They'll bring you down, and you'll never be at your best when you're down.

There's no room in any venture for a defeatist attitude. A lot of young people walk around thinking all the great ideas have been taken or that all the great projects have been started. But that's nonsense. There are opportunities all over the place. I think it was Daryl Zanuck who predicted the sure failure of television. He said nobody would be willing to sit in a living room and watch a plywood box; they'd rather go to the movies. Before that, there was somebody in 1925, right ahead of talkies, who said that nobody would pay to hear actors talk on film. At the turn of the century, the head of the U.S. Patent Office was quoted in the newspaper as stating that everything that could be invented had already been invented. All through history, people have acted as if there were nothing new, only those were the people who'd hit the end of their road. But they didn't necessarily hit the end of *your* road.

The barriers to entry in any field are the ones you put up for yourself. There's always plenty of room at the top. The middle can get pretty crowded. The bottom can get pretty crowded. But at the top there's always room. I have about 1,500 employees at FOX News, and every day I'm searching for a new producer. For someone great. Any one of my producers can step up at any time, and occasionally one of them does. And when that happens, I find a place for them in a heartbeat.

The other important thing I tell people is to be nice. It sounds so simple, but you'd be surprised how rare that is these days. People respond to you if they get the feeling you respond to them. If you're polite and businesslike. If you don't throw your position around. If you take the time to talk to people and actually listen. In every office, in every field, your colleagues can derail you if they don't like you. But if they like you, if they're pulling for you, things tend to work out just fine.

THREE

LEARNING BY EXAMPLE

Rudeness is the weak man's imitation of strength.

—ERIC HOFFER

My parents worked very hard to keep us kids grounded. But they didn't want us to feel entitled, even though they themselves were certainly entitled to a life filled with bells and whistles. The difference was that they'd worked for it and we had merely been born to it, and to their thinking that was all the difference in the world.

I don't think I fully appreciated the distinction back then. In fact, I'm sure I didn't, yet from the outset my brothers and I were made to realize that the luxuries we enjoyed were ours only in a once-removed sort of way. It turned out to be an excellent parenting strategy—although I can't say for certain that there was any real strategy. Mostly, it was a reflection of my parents' personalities and values, to reinforce for their children that we would have to work for that type of lifestyle. They put out the message that all those fine things were there for the taking but we would have to reach for them; nothing would be handed to us.

It was certainly a different approach. It made us stand apart in our social circle. A lot of my friends would talk about their private jets or

49

villas or yachts or their very latest toys and gadgets. Whenever they'd describe those extravagances, it was with a sense of ownership and prerogative—as in *my* jet, *my* villa, *my* yacht, *my* stuff. In our house, there was no room for that type of thinking. Yes, we got to enjoy a great many of the finer things in life, but it was always made clear to us that we were doing so at my parents' pleasure. They'd go out of their way to remind us of it at every turn. Not because they weren't generous people—they were. Not because they didn't want to share their good fortune with their children—they did. But they knew that if their teenage daughter grew up thinking she owned a casino or a yacht or a luxury apartment, it might mess with her head.

My parents were bottom-line-type people, and this was the bottom line.

When I was old enough to figure things out for myself, I admired my parents for their approach, but I don't think it was ever anything they sat down and discussed. We kids were just left to take in the message by osmosis—like the time we were leaving for a vacation in the south of France when I was about fourteen or fifteen and my mother handed me and my brothers our coach-class tickets before boarding the plane.

"Have a great flight," she said.

"You're not flying with us?" I asked. This was news to me.

"Of course I am," she said. "But I'll be up in first class. You and your brothers will be back in coach. Make sure to behave yourselves."

At the time, I thought this was the most spectacularly unfair development in the history of transatlantic travel. I couldn't understand it—and I fought it at first. I came to admire my parents' approach a little late. As my brothers will tell you, I was by far the most spoiled of the three of us. (This is still true, I'm afraid!) Despite my parents' best efforts to keep our heads in check, we inevitably enjoyed some luxuries from time to time—and I guess that, as a Trump, I'd begun to think of them as our due. So I complained to my mother about those particular travel arrangements, right there in the gate area. It seemed so unjust, so arbitrary, and I launched into my version of a temper tantrum. I said, "That's totally not fair. Why do you get to fly first class?"

I might have stamped my feet in protest but knew better.

My mother had a ready response. She said, "You're modeling now, Ivanka. If you want to spend some of your modeling money and upgrade your ticket, that would be great. In fact, I'd love the company. Otherwise, I'll be up in first class all by myself, with no one to talk to."

At that, I shut up and retreated to the back of the plane with my brothers. (As I recall, I was stuck in the middle seat between them, which ratcheted my indignation to a whole other level.) My mother was right, of course. I was making money as a model—not a lot yet but some. Already my parents were encouraging me to manage my money in age-appropriate ways, such as setting up my own bank account and monitoring my statements. Make no mistake, I wanted to enjoy first-class comforts, but not so much that I was willing to pay for them. Not with my own money, anyway.

KNOWLEDGE IS POWER

One area where my parents were happy to spend lavishly on their children was education, but that was a different type of expenditure as far as they were concerned. It wasn't about pampering us or indulging us or spoiling us in any way. It was an investment in our future. It was about seeking the very best, encouraging us to be the very best, and allowing us to inhabit an environment where we could do and be just that. It was part of their responsibility as parents, they believed. As long as our grades were good enough, we would go to the most prestigious private schools on the planet.

In my case, this meant Chapin, an exclusive all-girls prep school on Manhattan's Upper East Side. Then, in high school, I transferred to Choate Rosemary Hall, a prominent boarding school in Connecticut. If Chapin and Choate had been airline seats, they would have been first class all the way. Their reputations were well earned. My parents didn't see my enrollment there—or my brothers' at their fine schools—as any kind of indulgence. They wanted their children to be taught by the most inspiring teachers, surrounded by bright, motivated students from high-achieving families where success was expected. It was a given, in our house, that we would reach for the very top rungs of the private school ladder and, looking back, I suppose my father assessed the accompanying tuition bills in much the same way he looked at construction costs. He always used the finest materials, the top architects, the very best of everything when he was developing a new project. Each tower was built on a solid foundation, just as a first-tier education would fortify our foundations as individuals. Not that we couldn't get a perfectly fine education in a public school setting. Not that my father couldn't construct a perfectly respectable building using bricks instead of steel and glass. But he wanted the best for his children so that we might realize our full potential, and it ran to our extracurricular pursuits as well: ballet classes, piano lessons, French tutors . . .

From time to time, my sideline interests collided head-on with my parents' desire to provide as much as possible for their children. And somewhere in the pileup was whatever was left of my desire to have a normal childhood. That was always a big deal to me when I was little—to be just like everyone else, the kids whose parents weren't being written about in the tabloids—but, alas, normal wasn't always possible. Not in our house. Once, when I was around eight, I was fortunate enough to be admitted to the School of American Ballet, based in Lincoln Center. It was considered a great accomplishment to be accepted into this program, but I sometimes wonder if my application was helped along by my last name. Maybe, maybe not. I was good but not great. Focused, but not as single-minded as some of my tutu-wearing peers. And quite possibly too tall to make it as a ballerina. In any case, we were very young and extremely full of our little dancer selves. Such prima donnas! And it wasn't just the kids who took the program seriously. The instructors and choreographers approached each session as if the very future of American ballet rested on our performances. The highlight of our season was a performance of *The Nutcracker*. We rehearsed for months and months.

During that time, Michael Jackson was living one floor below us in Trump Tower. This was back when he was the undisputed "King of Pop," probably one of the most recognized and beloved entertainers in the world, at the height of his celebrity. You couldn't turn on the radio without hearing one of his hits or the television without seeing one of his videos. It certainly wasn't normal to have Michael Jackson as your neighbor, but it wasn't so awful, either. In fact, it was very cool, but even cool has its limits.

Somehow Michael heard about the looming *Nutcracker* performance and expressed an interest in attending. It's possible he was just being polite—but knowing Michael's affinity for dance, I think it's more likely that he was genuinely interested. So my father arranged to get him a ticket.

When the day of the performance finally came around, it appeared that word had gotten out that Michael Jackson was planning to attend. That, too, was cool—until word got around that *I* had had something to do with it. Naturally, the kids were over-the-top excited. I was also excited, but less so as the performance approached. You see, one of the older dancers had the idea that we should each wear a single white glove on our left hand as we danced *The Nutcracker*, to honor Michael. Cute and harmless, right? But I didn't see it that way. In fact, I was mortified. I was convinced that the sideshow would compromise the sanctity of *The Nutcracker* and that I would be singled out as the one to blame.

As it happened, the instructors shared my concern. In fact, they were furious and demanded to know who was responsible for undermining their otherwise estimable production. The teenage dancer and her friends who'd actually concocted the idea were too cowardly to fess up. All the grown-ups were running around backstage, frantic and crazy in their terribly important way, and I was certain that one of them would decide that I was the person responsible for the mess.

For a short-lived moment I wished like hell that I had been born into some other set of circumstances—far away from the spotlight I couldn't help but think was aimed at me, even when it wasn't. Happily, no one thought to blame me. The anger fizzled. We danced our little butts off. *The Nutcracker* emerged unscathed. Life went on in our precious little corner of New York City. And now, looking back, it's such a sweet, uniquely personal memory of such an iconic entertainer, even though at the time I tossed a whole lot of unnecessary adolescent angst into the mix.

P.S. Michael loved the show.

GET OUT OF TOWN

My parents believed that travel was a big part of my education, and they were only too happy to fund that aspect of my upbringing as well. It was mostly my mother's influence. My father is much more of a homebody; if it were up to him, he'd seldom leave New York. (He's always saying it's the greatest city in the world!) His idea of a perfect evening is to watch football in his Trump Tower penthouse. Even when he travels, he likes a controlled environment, which was why he always preferred to visit one of his own properties, like his Mar-a-Lago club in Palm Beach or one of his golf courses in New York or New Jersey. My mother is a whole other story. She loves a night on the town in Paris or San Tropez, a wild shopping spree in Milan, or a glamorous mountain adventure in the Alps—and I suppose that's understandable, considering how she was raised, in such a restrictive society. Now that she's able to see all those fabulous places—from such a lofty vantage point, no less—she's determined to take full advantage.

Good for her, I used to think. And, as it turned out, good for me, too, because I was one of her favorite traveling companions. We went everywhere together—sometimes with my brothers, sometimes just the two of us. All through childhood, there was one adventure after another to typical jet-setting-type hot spots, remote, undiscovered haunts, and everywhere in between. My childhood summers spent globetrotting with my mother gave me a tremendous worldview—all part of the well-rounded education my parents afforded me, the foundation they were laying for my future. I went to France, China, Argentina, Egypt . . . My mother would get excited about some part of the world she'd never seen or experienced, and off we'd go. It was wonderful! Outrageous, really. It was a special time alone with my mother and a chance to soak up her worlds of high style and high adventure—a special, boundless blessing all around.

Here, I guess, there were no lessons to be learned by making me travel coach, especially since I was too young on a lot of these trips to be traveling unaccompanied. We definitely spent a lot of time in five-star hotels and first-class restaurants—my mother was not one to rough it!—but we always managed to do some exploring at ground level, and somewhere along the way I became aware that the world was filled with interesting, intellectual, passionate, and incredibly dynamic people who had never heard of Chapin and Choate, people who'd never been inside one of my dad's buildings, people who didn't seem attached in any way to the social conventions that marked my days back home.

I'll say this: I caught the travel bug in a big way. So much so that I've probably shot past my mother by now. It's gotten to the point where my passport is one of my most cherished possessions—for both the reminder it offers of the places I've been and the open book it represents for all the trips still to come. I consider it a diploma, of a kind, alongside the one I received from Wharton; it signals a real accomplishment and a profound education. I've kept a running count of all the countries I've visited, and as of this writing I'm past one hundred. Most people I know can't even *name* a hundred different countries, let alone claim any firsthand experience of them—and here again I don't mean to strut, just to emphasize the precious gifts I was given and to encourage all to reach for their own version of the same experience. Whatever you can afford, in terms of time and money, I'd say go for it. Get away, wherever you can, whenever you can, even if it means back-packing across the country or vagabonding between European youth hostels. Expose yourself to something new. Taste and see and feel what you can. Think of it like an investment, because your experiences are bound to deliver a healthy return at some point.

I've come to believe that the better rounded and more open-minded you are, the more strongly you'll perform in any business set-ting. The more experiences you have, the more experiences you'll be able to call on in any number of circumstances. Remember, being suc-cessful in business isn't just about crunching numbers or being profi-cient in Excel. The single best indicator of your success starting out will be your ability to relate to other people—your boss, your clients, and your coworkers. Traveling is probably the best way I know to learn to interact with others, to boost your confidence in unfamiliar set-tings, and to improve your people skills. When you have to communi-cate with people who might not speak your language or share your customs, it forces you to break out of your shell and adapt. It lifts you out of your routine.

Travel has undoubtedly made me a much stronger entrepreneur. And it's opened up a world of opportunities for the growth of the Trump Organization—literally. Before my brothers and I joined the company, our business was primarily a New York–based operation. "There are plenty of great deals right here in New York," my father used to say, although he didn't need us to push him to explore projects in Atlantic City, Chicago, Florida, or elsewhere in the United States. He strongly believes that a developer should not build in a market that he doesn't fully understand or visit frequently. That's where my brothers and I come in. Our love of travel has opened the door to a world of deals—in every sense of the term. Since I joined the company in 2005, my job has taken me to countries such as Panama, Colombia, Jordan, Israel, and a number of other exciting places where I've had to conduct business alongside unique sets of customs, perspectives, and politics.

I've had no choice but to adapt. Before each trip, I immerse myself in the local culture. I read everything I can get my hands on. I reach out to contacts and associates who have done business in the area. I'm determined not to be one of those ugly Americans who leaves her hotel only for meetings and eats only room-service hamburgers. I get out and soak in what I can.

A WORLD OF OPPORTUNITY

Not too long ago, I was in Almaty, Kazakhstan, for a meeting with prospective business partners. One night I was taken out to a dinner where I was served two local specialties: *besbarmak,* boiled horse meat, and *shubat,* fermented camel's milk. Not surprisingly, my first instinct was to gag, but I'd been offered far worse on previous trips—*chou dofu* ("stinky tofu") in Taiwan and *surströmming* (fermented herring) in Sweden—so I dug right in. I didn't get very far with the horse meat. In fact, I couldn't bring myself to take a bite, but I took pains to disguise my lack of interest from my hosts. I did manage a few polite sips of the camel's milk, which seemed to please my hosts immensely. If I'd freaked out and pushed my plate away, I would have embarrassed my hosts and potentially damaged a relationship I'd flown halfway around the world to strengthen. Sampling (almost) everything they had to offer demonstrated respect—the one true global currency.

The more you travel, the more open you are to whatever comes your way, and this was never more apparent than on my very first business trip as a member of the Trump Organization. I'd been at the company for about two weeks when I flew to Dubai with my brother Don to explore a potential deal. By now many of us have seen the breathtaking development of the Palm Jumeirah island, but at the time there were just renderings of the grand development plan. It was all very pie in the sky and impossible to fathom. The renderings were like some city of the future you might see on display at Epcot or on the Discovery Channel, the way the buildings seemed to just flower up out of the ocean. But as I toured the area and met all the people involved, I started to realize that it was no city of the future. It was no grand delusion. It was real. I visited with the developers. I studied the plans. I met the engineers. I saw the dredging efforts firsthand.

My first thought was, How in the world am I ever going to be able to explain this to my father? Structurally speaking, a project like that had never been attempted. Practically speaking, the plans made no sense. Financially speaking . . . I couldn't even begin to attach a price tag to this vision. To dump millions of tons of sand into the middle of the sea, to create all that spectacular beach frontage and artificial islands and a platform for a real-life city of the future? It was completely unfeasible, unworkable. Yet it was real and tangible and well on its way—close enough to touch. Those talented, visionary developers were determined to make the impossible possible, and I left the United Arab Emirates certain they could pull it off. I was also confident that the project presented a big opportunity for us, one that didn't require any real financial risk. All the developers wanted from us was our name and managerial expertise—to brand one of their signature towers, which was scheduled to be built after the first phase of the resort's construction was complete—and they were willing to pay handsomely for it.

The entire flight home, I ran through different scenarios in my head, trying to think how I might pitch the project to my father without his throwing me out of his office and wondering why he'd hired me. It was probably too big to be my first deal, and it was certainly too bizarre. Nobody had ever done anything like it before. At home. Abroad. Anywhere. Nobody in their right mind with any experience in development would even consider doing anything like it, but it was getting done—with us or without us. Trouble was, it was one of those deals where you had to see it to believe it. I didn't think my words or power of description could ever do the plans justice.

On that trip, I was staying at the Burj Al Arab, which had quickly become the gold standard hotel in Dubai, and I was blown away by the architecture of the place. Here again, the structure made little sense—a massive building with a vast open space carved into its middle in such a way that a substantial amount of the interior space was unusable. Glorious but unusable. I stood dumbstruck in the hotel lobby, trying to take a picture of the amazing ceiling, like a wide-eyed tourist. But before I could snap the shutter, I was rushed by a mob of burly men dressed in traditional white robes, their heads covered. I was terrified, of course, but then I put two and two together and realized the men were security guards, trying to prevent me from taking a picture. The reason? They were protecting a Saudi sheik, and they thought my camera had been pointed in his direction. The sheik had been standing in the bar—and he couldn't have his picture taken in a bar, because Sharia law prohibits drinking. I suppose I knew that, on some level, but it never occurred to me that he was in my shot as I pointed the camera or that I was causing any trouble. Over time, I'd learn to anticipate such faux pas. There, especially, I should have known better. You see, everyone in the Muslim world goes to Dubai to party. But in Islamic law, drinking is unacceptable, which I guess means that whatever happens in Dubai is meant to stay in Dubai.

Like Vegas, only more so.

I made my sheepish apologies and returned to my property tour, none the worse for wear, but if I hadn't been a relatively seasoned traveler I might have been too flustered to continue on about my business.

As it happened, Don and I found a way to make a believable pitch to my father once we got home—a tip: when words fail, use photos, architectural renderings, and engineering studies whenever possible—and we ended up licensing our name to the project. It hasn't been completed yet, but in presales Trump International Hotel & Tower, Dubai, has generated the highest price per square foot in the region by a factor of three! Not bad for my first deal.

THE END OF SOMETHING

When I was nine years old, my parents sat me down and explained that they were having problems in their relationship. They had the same conversation with my brothers. They spoke to each of us separately and as a family; they addressed our concerns together, as a couple, and individually. They surrounded the issue from every conceivable angle. Except one: none of us kids had seen it coming.

Even at such a young age, I knew what it meant. A lot of my friends were children of divorce, but when my parents announced that they were separating, I felt sure it was only a temporary situation. It was just a hiccup, I thought. Something to get past. After all, I'd rarely ever seen them exchange harsh words or raise their voices. There was no tension around our dinner table—at least none that I could pick up on. Whatever it was, I was confident they would work things out, so I listened politely to their rehearsed explanations and then went about my business.

Later that week, I was walking to school past a newsstand when I saw a tabloid headline screaming at me from the front page of the Daily News: "LOVE ON THE ROCKS." Right there, for all the world to see—in big, bold letters alongside a picture of my parents that looked as if it had been torn down the middle. It was devastating, mortifying, violating to see an intensely private matter on display in such a weirdly public way.

I was so young, so naive, that I had just assumed that things between my parents would be fine—until I was confronted with that front-page bulletin. I wanted to run and hide, but of course I couldn't because I was walking with my friends and I didn't want to add to my embarrassment. It was the beginning of a tension-filled period in our lives that shook me up in a big way. It wasn't just the fact that my parents were really and truly splitting up that I had to consider. It was the fact that my family life was now open to such close, harsh inspection. My parents had been so careful to talk to me and my brothers about their marriage in a loving, age-appropriate way. They were both very smart, media-savvy people, but I don't think either one of them saw the magnitude of what was coming.

That *Daily News* headline was just the first of many. For a couple of months, there was some aspect of my parents' breakup being played out on the front pages of the tabloids almost every day. Someone told me years later that my parents' breakup and the ensuing fallout was the longest-running front-page story in tabloid history until the O. J. Simpson trial. I don't know if that's true, but it did seem as if the media's appetite for the story was insatiable. One day the headline was "THEY MET IN CHURCH!" The next it was "SEPARATE BEDS!" The worst was a *New York Post* cover photo of Marla Maples, a woman I'd never met, who was being talked about as my father's new girlfriend, claiming that she had spent the night with my father beneath a headline that shouted, "THE BEST SEX I EVER HAD!"

Can you imagine?

It got to where I couldn't walk to school, go to the park, visit my friends, or move about anywhere in public because reporters were camped out all along my usual paths. They were so aggressive, so ruthless. Every day, I'd have to pass a gauntlet of photographers out in front of my school, waiting to get a picture of me. They'd shout my name as I passed or ask some horribly inappropriate question, just to get me to turn my head in their direction. The day after that *New York Post* cover, one idiot reporter even had the temerity to ask me if Marla Maples's claims were true. What type of person would ask a nine-year-old girl that kind of question? About her own father, no less?

But we were fair game, our lives on full display. And the questions kept coming. Did I like Marla? Whom did I want to live with after the divorce? Was my mother seeing anyone? It was so insane, so offensive, so upsetting. And there was no let-up.

My dad had moved out, but together my parents tried to protect us as best they could. If we were watching television and a tabloid-type show was about to come on, they'd change the channel. If there was a copy of *People* lying around the house that might have a story about the divorce, they'd throw it out before we could read it. They did everything they could to limit our exposure to the story—but of course they couldn't do everything. It took on a life of its own, beyond anyone's control.

Somehow my parents managed to be civil to each other in our presence, through the very worst of it. They never fought in front of us. In fact, they went out of their way to keep things pleasant and loving and on an even keel. Despite all the tension and animosity and difficulties that had apparently surfaced between them, we never heard either parent say a bad word about the other. We never heard a door slam. And we were never put into a position where we'd have to pick sides.

It was a healthy approach to an unhealthy situation.

If there was a silver lining to that ugly, uncertain time, it was that my parents' divorce brought me and my brothers much closer together. Before all of it, we were just like any other set of siblings: we bickered, we tolerated one another, but that was it. Now, though, we'd been forced into us-versus-the-world mode. The divorce, the media swirl, and the general upheaval in our little lives thrust us together in such a way that we responded as a unit, bonded with one another in a whole new way.

The divorce also brought me closer to my father. Not because I was taking his side but because I could no longer take him for granted. Before the divorce, whenever he came home from work I'd run over to him and give him a quick kiss and then race back to whatever I'd been doing. That changed once he moved out. He didn't move all that far away, just a few floors below us. But now I went down to see him every morning before school, and I also started dropping by his office on my way home in the afternoon. Just to say hello. In no hurry to get back to whatever I'd been doing, because nothing was more important.

Not incidentally, all that time in my father's office was well spent. I went to hang out and spend time with him, but I couldn't help but soak up a thing or two about business. The language of the deal, the language of construction, the language of the workplace . . . it all became a part of me, without my even realizing it.

Even though the divorce changed my relationship with my brothers and my parents for the better, it was still the darkest, most difficult period in my young life—not least because it coincided with two devastating losses. The first: my grandfather Dedo died at the height of all this craziness. His death was hard on all of us, my brothers especially. They'd had a special relationship with him, and to lose the stability, love, and friendship he offered, at a time when we were also worried that we might be losing our father, was a staggering blow.

The second: shortly after Dedo died, my nanny Bridget Carroll passed away. Bridget's death was also a serious blow, but now it was my turn to be hardest hit. She'd been like a second mother to me, my closest confidant, and now it felt as if I needed her warmth and wisdom all the more. Losing Bridget and Dedo so close together, in the middle of so much family turmoil, sent me reeling.

Despite all the pain I felt at the time, I got through it. Surviving those low moments certainly helped shape the person I am today. I firmly believe that without those heartaches, my life might have been just a little too easy. Really, all I'd ever known up to that point was privilege and contentment. About the worst I'd had to deal with was a little embarrassment over that Michael Jackson–inspired *Nutcracker* incident—or some other relatively inconsequential calamity. In a way, I needed those tumultuous days to give my life shape and meaning and to reinforce the all-important point that there were some difficulties money couldn't fix and celebrity couldn't smooth over.

A series of setbacks like the ones I experienced in 1990 can either break you or make you stronger. I was only nine years old, and the fallout from my parents' divorce would continue into my middle school years, but I chose to gain strength from this period. And to move on.

JONATHAN TISCH—Chairman and CEO, Loews Hotels; Co-chairman, Loews Corporation

ON PERSPECTIVE

In today's hospitality business, it's harder than ever to stand out. All hotels have nice lobbies, new bedding, and flat-screen TVs, so it's the attention to detail that creates memorable experiences for our guests and allows Loews Hotels to differentiate itself from the competition.

To execute that level of expertise fully requires buy-in from all levels at the company. I can make all the decisions I want about the future of Loews Hotels from my office in midtown Manhattan, but day in and day out I'm not the one on the front lines interacting with our guests. That's an invaluable perspective, yet it's often out of reach for most executives. However, a couple of years ago I had an opportunity to go back and do the critical jobs that truly make us successful. The opportunity came about through a show on TLC (The Learning Channel) called *Now Who's Boss?* In it, CEOs are put to work in entry-level positions in their own companies. For one week at Loews Miami Beach Hotel, I worked as a house-keeper, front desk clerk, bellman, short-order cook, pool attendant, and several other positions. Having grown up in the industry, I'd worked in all these jobs as a young person, but I had never done them after becoming CEO. It was a very valuable and meaningful way to remind myself how difficult the work is and how important those team members are to our overall effort. It gave me a new appreciation for the attention to detail necessary for our company's success.

Another important perspective, particularly when you work in a family business, is an outsider's point of view. A family business presents its own share of challenges, and it helps to come to it after spending time at another company, even in another industry. Rather than return to New York City and join Loews Hotels after graduating from Tufts University in 1976, I decided to stay in Boston and spent the next three years working at WBZ-TV. My experiences as a cameraman, editor, and producer were invaluable and gave me a sense of self as well as an opportunity to work in an industry where nobody cared if my last name was Tisch, Trump, or Smith. My time working in television taught me many important lessons about the responsibilities that go along with having a job and about presenting an image, telling a story, and focusing on details.

That's why I always tell young people to free themselves up when they think about their first job. It can be anything. It doesn't even have to be related to what you've studied in college. You never know where life is going to take you or how what you're doing might translate to what you'll do next. The outside perspective I gained in television continues to pay dividends more than thirty years later. I now host my own television program and make good and frequent use of my media training to help promote Loews Hotels and the travel and tourism industry at large. Ultimately, that's been the great lesson for me, to be open to different perspectives. Learning from other people and from every experience will play a part in your own success.

FOUR

CREATING VALUES

The reasonable man adapts himself to the world, the
unreasonable one persists in trying to adapt the world to
himself. Therefore, all progress depends on the unreasonable.

—GEORGE BERNARD SHAW

My parents might have placed a special emphasis on our education
and travel, but neither aspect of my childhood would have made much
of a dent without the emphasis they also placed on hard work and
dedication. No matter what we were doing, we were meant to do it to
the best of our ability. And to pitch in. My brothers and I never really
had a set list of chores we were meant to complete. Our household was
too busy, too crazy for any kind of predictable routine. But if one of us
was ever asked to do the dishes after dinner or put away the laundry,
we were expected to do it right away, no questions asked.

I probably groaned a time or two at those demands on my precious teenage time, but I was smart enough to make sure no one heard
me. My brothers, too. We had it pretty good, and if that meant taking
out the trash every once in a while, we knew to do so with reasonably
good cheer. My parents had both been raised to follow orders, and
they expected us to do so as well. They even expected us to volunteer
to help without being prompted—another tall order for restless, in-
tractable kids—but we figured out what we needed to do to stay in our

parents' good graces, a step or two ahead of their expectations. If we were obstinate or rolled our eyes in a discernible way, my mother was quick to point out how lucky we were. Compared to her own spartan childhood in Communist Czechoslovakia, this was readily apparent. When she was a little girl, there had been no money for fancy clothes or new toys. Actually, even if there had been money, there were no stores in Czechoslovakia that sold those things at the time. Most people struggled just to get by, and children were expected to work very hard and pull their own weight. That was the norm. Everybody did without and appreciated what they had. That a child would disobey her parents or complain about doing chores was unheard of.

My father grew up in a far more privileged environment, but his parents were careful to keep him focused and grounded. They didn't always get things right, but they tried. There's one story my father likes to tell about how my grandfather used to drive him to school in his Rolls-Royce, but instead of dropping him off at the front entrance he'd deposit him at the nearest subway station. Then my father would travel the rest of the way by subway. I always found this story both odd and endearing. I get the lesson my grandfather was trying to teach, but it seemed almost beside the point. I mean, my father was still being driven to school in a Rolls-Royce each morning—just not *all the way* to school. But that was the contradiction of growing up with the Trump name, even for my father.

Actually, my grandfather had a lot of ideas on how to instill positive values and a strong work ethic in his children. He also put a great many of them into play with me and my brothers. When I was little, he used to flash a bright, shiny silver dollar and ask, "Would you like this, Ivanka?"

I never knew where he got all those shiny new coins, but he always seemed to have a ready supply. And of course I'd nod or smile or jump up and down.

"Well," he'd say, "before I can give it to you, you need to ask your grandmother if she has any chores for you to do."

Then I'd find my grandmother and see if she needed any help, at which point she'd usually ask me to set the table or sweep the floor or help her mash the potatoes for dinner. When I was through, I'd go back to my grandfather and report on my efforts.

"Very good," he'd say, handing over the silver dollar. "This is for all your hard work. You've earned it."

He made it into a game, but his message was clear: if you want something, you have to work for it. There weren't going to be any handouts in the Trump family.

LIVE TO WORK, WORK TO LIVE

As we got older, my brothers and I were expected to work at different Trump properties. When I was fifteen, my summer job was to shadow the foreman during the construction of Trump World Tower, an amazing eighty-nine-story complex my father was building right next to the United Nations. It was my first day-to-day exposure to construction, and I absolutely loved it. Everything about building seemed so exciting, so interesting, so momentous. I even enjoyed the language of the job site. (Where else do you get to use words like *joist* and *rebar*?) And I loved the fact that we were all pitching in to build something that would permanently alter the skyline of the city—hopefully, in a positive and profitable way.

For many summers, my brother Don worked at the Trump Marina in Atlantic City, mooring boats to the dock all day for minimum wage. Another summer, Eric worked on the landscaping crew at Seven Springs, our country estate in Bedford, New York. Whatever he had us doing, my father believed it was important for us to do hands-on work of some kind or other. He wanted us to get to know the people and the processes that actually made our company run, from the ground up. Even when we were kids, there was talk around the dinner table about how we all might join the family business some day. It wasn't demanded of us. And it wouldn't be handed to us. But my father put it out there as something we might want to work toward. Or not. We would work toward something, that much was certain. And since we would likely spend most of our adult lives working in an office and dealing with lawyers and financiers, my father figured our teenage years offered the first and last and best chance for us to get our hands dirty. His thinking was that once we saw how much sweat and effort went into completing and maintaining a Trump property, we'd have a better appreciation for the people who helped to make our business successful. As a bonus, we'd learn the value of an honest day's work.

GIVE-AND-TAKE

I learned early on not to ask my parents for anything they might have reasonably expected me to pay for myself—or to do without. I strayed from this lesson at my own peril, like the time I stopped by my father's office after school with my good friend Lysandra. We were about to leave for a weekend with her family in Newport, Rhode Island, so I asked my father if I could use his credit card to buy a new bathing suit for the trip. A new bathing suit I certainly didn't need.

(Hey, you can't blame a girl for trying!)

Sure enough, my father wasn't at all interested in handing over his credit card just so I could buy yet another swimsuit. "Ivanka," he said firmly, "you get plenty of money for new clothes. I'm sure the suits you already have are just fine."

He was right, they were. But that wasn't the point. Lysandra's father had just given her *his* credit card for a new bathing suit, and we wanted to go off on a little shopping spree before we left. *That* was the point. I knew deep down I'd get nowhere with my father, but I kept at it. I motioned to my friend—Exhibit A. "Lysandra's father gave her his card," I said feebly. The moment I said it, I realized I had played my cards badly.

My father shook his head slightly. Then he turned to my friend and asked, "Lysandra, do you really think you need a new bathing suit?"

And that was that. I'd been defeated.

Eventually I learned not to ask for too many indulgences—not because I'd figured out that it wouldn't get me anywhere but because I came to see that my father was right. I didn't deserve the excesses, I realized, and in some ways I diminished myself by asking for them. My father was only too happy to cover my basic needs and even a few luxuries from time to time. But being turned down more often than not, I learned to appreciate the gifts and extravagances I did receive. My parents wanted to make sure that I wouldn't be one of those poor little rich kids, drowning in excess and never learning the true value of a dollar. Not if they played it right. And they did.

As I said, my parents stood apart in this approach. A lot of my friends came from wealthy families. It was part of the package at schools like Chapin and Choate—and it was a running theme among my girlfriends, in a great many of our adolescent conversations, how someone's Draconian parents wouldn't cover her cell phone bill or, in more extreme cases, buy her a new car or a Cartier watch for graduation. There was a whole lot of whining and moaning, but you didn't usually hear that kind of noise from me or my brothers. Whether by design or happy accident, my parents created an atmosphere in our house in which we kids felt foolish asking for things we hadn't earned—and somewhat ashamed.

Make no mistake, I wanted and appreciated the same nice things my friends wanted and appreciated. It's just that I came to look on them as a kind of carrot, an incentive for me to do well enough that I would be able to afford to buy whatever it was that I wanted for myself. My friends just wanted them. Right away. On a silver platter, I guess. Somehow my parents had me thinking I should be self-sufficient, and for as long as I can remember I've never been comfortable relying on someone else to provide for me. I knew my parents would always be there for me if I were ever up against it—but I wasn't planning on being up against it.

These days, it's a point of pride that I'm in control of my own life.

I own a two-bedroom apartment in a Trump building, but no one gave it to me. Nor did I benefit from an insider price. I bought my first apartment in one of our buildings because I believe in the Trump brand and in the value of an investment in one of our properties. I'm paying a mortgage on my apartment, just as my brothers, Don and Eric, pay mortgages on their apartments in other Trump buildings. Admittedly, I pay my mortgage directly to my father instead of to a bank, but it's a mortgage just the same, and I've never missed a payment.

That said, some of my friends learn about this arrangement and scratch their heads. Either they don't believe me or they don't get why my father wouldn't just give me an apartment, and I have a hard time explaining it. In truth, he probably would let me live for free in one of our buildings, but only temporarily. He wouldn't just *give* me an apartment, and I wouldn't accept one if he did; I wouldn't want to be beholden to him in that way. Now, as an adult, I like the feeling of being able to provide for myself and of owning my own lifestyle. Plus, when I'm ready to move on I'd like to make a nice return on this particular real estate investment—just as our other residents do.

In this way, I suppose, I'm doing more than living up to my parents' standards; I'm living up to my own.

It's so interesting to me now that none of us kids looked to my father as an ATM machine. Even my little sister Tiffany—my father's daughter with his second wife, Marla Maples—understands that it's not acceptable, not necessary, not *cool* to ask my father for money all the time. Clearly, he must have been doing something right, but whatever it was, it was subtle. He never sat us down and lectured us about the value of a dollar or the importance of paying our own way. Yet the message came across clearly.

This past Christmas, Tiffany came to me with a dilemma. She'd moved to California with her mother when she was just seven years old, so she spent a whole lot less time with our father than we did. Now she was fifteen, and she wanted to know if there was a good way to approach our dad about her relatively simple money needs. Not because she was spoiled but because she was a teenager. If she'd been living in the same house with our father, she'd have been able to go up to him from time to time and ask for a little something extra. And he would have been inclined to give it to her, just as he'd given somewhat freely to me and my brothers whenever we'd asked him for a special treat. There were even times when he would just surprise us with a nice gift for no reason at all, on no special occasion, and I imagine Tiffany didn't get to enjoy the same surprises, just by virtue of lack of proximity.

A lot of Tiffany's friends had access to their parents' credit cards, she told me. Some had fixed spending limits. Some could just spend whatever they wanted until Daddy said otherwise, which basically meant whatever they could get away with. They all received excessive allowances, but that wasn't what Tiffany was looking for. All she wanted, really, was a way to enjoy some of the same privileges her friends got to enjoy, in the same way she would have enjoyed them if she'd lived under our father's roof. I certainly understood that. For all my talk about being independent as a kid, I'd been only too happy to spend my father's money from time to time—within reason, of course. I'd see a fun pair of earrings or a new bag that all my friends were carrying and reach for it. Not in a *think nothing of it* sort of way but in a *just this once* sort of way. I didn't run up thousands and thousands of dollars' worth of charges on my father's credit card. Not even hundreds and hundreds. I don't think I was overindulged as a kid. Just indulged. Just a little. And now Tiffany quite reasonably found herself in the same place, with no good way to ask our father for the same little bits of indulgence he'd shared with me and my brothers.

She had the strategy worked out for how she would ask him for an increased allowance. She'd given it a lot of thought, and she was nervous about approaching our father, so I tried to set her at ease. As she spoke I kept thinking how great it was, how sweet, that this type of thinking had somehow been passed along to Tiffany. I was so proud of her for being reluctant to ask but at the same time just trying to be like all the other girls in her crowd. And I was so proud of our dad for setting such a strong example and instilling such positive values about money in *all* of his children—even from such a long distance away.

The footnote to this story is that Big Sis did an end-around to save Tiffany the trouble. I didn't tell her, of course, but I went to our father and suggested he think about surprising Tiffany with a credit card for Christmas, with a small monthly allowance on it. Sure enough, he did just that. Tiffany was thrilled and relieved. And so appreciative. That made all the difference: we all appreciate what we have. We don't take advantage of it or expect it as our due.

And we certainly don't count on it.

GREAT EXPECTATIONS

My parents have both led nontraditional lifestyles—but they have extremely traditional relationships with their children. They might have taken me to boxing matches or on trips around the world, but at the end of the day they were always my parents, not my best friends.

Here, too, our relationship stood in stark contrast to the way my friends seemed to interact with their own parents. I had one friend in particular who would shout the most wildly disrespectful things at her mother whenever she didn't get her way. "Go to hell!" she'd scream. "Leave me alone!" I was always blown away, hearing her go off like that on her own mother. If I'd ever spoken that way to my mother, my butt would have been red for days. And if I'd ever spoken that way in front of other people—well, I still wouldn't be able to sit down, all these years later.

The disrespectful behavior, the sense of entitlement, the disinclination to work hard—it was all tied in. Thankfully, there wasn't a whole lot of that in our household. There was some but not a lot, and whenever one of those negatives leaked from me or my brothers, my parents put a quick end to it. We were all fast learners, so we seldom exhibited the same bad behavior a second time. It was all but inevitable, then, that a positive picture began to come into focus. My brothers and I turned out mostly okay, unlike a lot of children born into wealth and opportunity, and looking back I realize it was my parents' firm hand that kept us on such solid ground.

Growing up, I met far too many well-off kids who had a tough time finding their own way. A lot of them are still struggling as they turn the corner into their thirties. It's hard to get too concerned about a bunch of spoiled rich kids who could never quite get past their privileged childhoods, but if you're never taught to value hard work or strive for self-sufficiency, you'll never be in a position to take full advantage of your opportunities. For the most part, my friends who struggled the most were the ones with the biggest and most unencumbered trust funds, which usually meant there was no incentive for them to go it alone. Instead of making every effort to succeed, they made no effort at all.

Understand, it wasn't the trust fund itself that seemed to cause all the trouble for my contemporaries; it was the fact of its existence that tripped them up, along with the access to it. A lot of people don't believe me when I tell them there's no trust fund waiting for me somewhere down the road. I guess it's possible that my parents might have set one up for me, but they've never told me about it, and that's the key. It can't be healthy to grow up knowing you'll come into a large sum of money at a certain age. It can't instill in you an abiding work ethic or a burning desire to succeed. It's one thing to be surprised by a windfall inheritance, and quite another to count on it, because when you count on it you count yourself out. It's a blessing either way, no doubt about it, but it's more of a mixed blessing when it's held out in front of you. It encourages you to live *down* to everyone's expectations—because more often than not there are no expectations at all.

I have more friends than I care to count who've frittered away their young adulthoods on nothing much at all. Oh, they went through the motions and did what was minimally expected of them and graduated from college, but after that they tapped their toes and tapped their kegs and tapped their parents' patience and best intentions, waiting for some far-off day when they might gain control of their pot of gold. At this point they're not really friends, because there's no room in my life for people who can't seem to find any motivation in theirs. They're more like a sad collection of cautionary tales.

It's easy to chalk up this lack of ambition to laziness, but I believe there's another factor at work as well. A lot of my friends who are children of extremely successful parents have developed a consuming fear that they will never be able to match their parents' success. It's the weight of great expectations, on both sides, and I can certainly understand it. Frankly, I've felt it myself—only in my case I was given the tools and the encouragement I needed to conquer the weight of those expectations. Unfortunately, that's not always the case. You go to the finest schools, you're surrounded by the best minds, you have access to the kinds of connections that will help you get a running start in any endeavor, yet you can't shake thinking that you'll never live up to your parents' accomplishments or be taken seriously on your own merit. As a result, you fall into a kind of professional paralysis. I was able to get past it, but I'm one of the lucky ones. My brothers, too, although in our case I have to think it was more than luck. It was an extra push on the part of our parents, to ensure that our advantages didn't become a crutch or a salve.

A lot of these issues are explored in a compelling way in the documentary *Born Rich*, made by my friend Jamie Johnson. Jamie is one of the heirs to the Johnson & Johnson fortune, so he knows the territory, and his film explores how and why so many of his wealthy friends have struggled to come to terms with their families' success—and their stops and starts along the way. There's a lot to admire about this film and a lot we can learn from it, but as I watched it the first time I kept thinking how arrogant and ungrateful most of Jamie's subjects seemed to be. It's as if they were asking us to somehow feel sorry for them because they'd been dealt such a favorable hand.

Born Rich received a good deal of press when it was finally released, but when I filmed my segment I had only an idea of the documentary's subject matter. I was also under the impression that Jamie was taping the piece to fulfill a school assignment, so it never occurred to me that it would be widely released. Jamie was a friend of mine, so when he asked if he could come over with a camera crew and talk to me about what it was like to grow up in a wealthy family, I didn't think too much of it. In fact, I didn't hear from Jamie about it for several years. We did our interview, and that was that. I was eighteen at the time, and here's what I said: "No matter what I hear or read about my family, the fact is I'm absolutely proud to be a Trump. I'm proud of my family name and everything they've accomplished. For a while I worried that I'd always be under my parents' shadow, but I guess it's not a bad shadow to be under."

When it first aired on HBO several years later, a lot of critics and pundits weighed in about how shallow a lot of the kids appeared. People were quick to criticize the snobbish, loutish behavior Jamie had captured with his interviews—and for the most part the commentary was justified. Inevitably, I worried that I might be painted with the same brush. My thoughts were mixed in with everyone else's. But over time I began to notice that I wasn't catching much heat at all. If anything, people seemed to appreciate what I had to say about growing up in my parents' formidable shadows. I think viewers respected that I stood up for my family and showed real pride in what we've all accomplished. Not just my father. Not just my mother. All of us.

Sure, my parents cast a big shadow. Sure, their accomplishments can seem intimidating. But I never shrank from the standards they set. Instead, I've pushed myself even harder to fill all the spaces where their big shadows might not yet reach, to harness some of their power and influence and use it to propel myself forward in life. I tell myself that my father never shied away from trying to measure up to his own successful father; if anything, he was openly competing with my grandfather's legacy. I don't see it as a competition, but I do take it as a challenge, and I look ahead to the day when I can stand alongside my father as a true equal.

And when that happens—and it *will* happen—I know that he'll take great pride in what we've managed to achieve. All of us. Together.

CATHIE BLACK——President, Hearst Magazines

ON MAKING AN IMPRESSION

Young people today have had things happen easily for them, but at the same time they're very daunted by the business climate they're facing. I understand that, but what I don't get is why they don't take full advantage of the opportunities that continue to come their way. It's so important to make good and appropriate use of your contacts. Let's say you've arranged an interview through a family friend with someone who might be able to open a door for you. So many kids throw up their hands and say, "No, I'll do it on my own." I hear that and think, *Okay, it's great to want to be independent, but why turn down an assist?* If someone is willing to make a phone call or send an e-mail on your behalf, you should thank them profusely and see what happens. Meet with them, and see what happens. They're not going to find you a job. It's still up to you. But they might make things a little easier. They might get you to think about your career in a totally new way.

In the end, it's all about persistence and follow-through. It's about doing your research so you know what you're talking about. These are just the basics, but I'm afraid I don't see the basics anymore. I can't tell you how many people send me a letter or an e-mail, and they haven't checked how to spell my name. They haven't checked my title. They haven't checked the address. In an interview I might suggest they take some notes, but then they'll fish around for a pen or pull out some ratty piece of paper. I see that and tell them to invest in a nice leather-bound portfolio. Have a lined pad inside it. Print up a set of business cards; it'll cost you only about ten dollars. And be sure to bring a copy of your résumé. I know you've already sent one, but it doesn't matter. Have another one handy. Maybe the person you're meeting with never got it or misplaced it or would like another copy to share with a colleague.

Be prepared. Again, it's so basic. Do a little bit of research on the person you're calling on and the company he or she works for. Google him or her. Personally, I never take a meeting or see someone for lunch if I haven't Googled that person first. The information is out there, so you might as well use it. The idea is that if someone is giving you twenty minutes of their valuable time, you should maximize that investment. Make good use of their time and yours. Be as informed as you possibly can about the individual, about the product, the service. Know everything you can going in. It's not as if you're there for twenty minutes just to pick that person's brain. You're there to gain insight or information that you can't find anywhere else—and, hopefully, to grow this one contact into others. I always tell young people to try to close those types of meetings by getting the names of at least three other people they can reach out to, hopefully with an introduction.

More than anything else, you're there to make an impression, so you'll do well to realize that first impressions are lasting impressions. It's not just about how you carry yourself when you walk through the door. It's not just about how well spoken you are or whether you have to go searching through your bag just to find a pen and some paper. And it's not even about wearing designer clothes and wowing the person across the table with your sense of style. It's about looking professional and appropriate. If you're meeting with someone at an advertising agency, go ahead and dress creatively, but if you're headed to a law firm, be sure to dress conservatively.

And realize you'll make a first impression before you even arrive for your meeting. I recently gave a college commencement address and looked on from the stage as one of the professors introduced the school's salutatorian. The dean listed all of this young woman's accomplishments, and then, in a joking aside, he asked, "And would you like to know what's on her Facebook page?"

I could see the student only from the back, but I thought she was going to have a heart attack. She turned and flashed the dean a look that seemed to say, "How did you get on my Facebook page?" But it's out there, of course. If you've put up pictures of yourself dancing topless and drinking your little head off, they're out there for all to see. You can't get all indignant if a professor or a potential employer seeks out your Facebook or Twitter or MySpace account. You can't say, "Well, you shouldn't be looking at that." If you're an employer and you have a choice of ten applicants or one hundred and ten, you're going to choose the one who keeps her shirt on. End of story.

FIVE

MODELING A CAREER

Nothing in the world can take the place of persistence. Talent
will not; nothing is more common than unsuccessful men
with talent. Genius will not; unrewarded genius is almost
a proverb. Education alone will not; the world is full of
educated derelicts. Persistence and determination alone are
omnipotent. The slogan "press on" has solved and always
will solve the problems of the human race.

—CALVIN COOLIDGE

It was never a question that I would work for a living. It was hardly
even a question what I would do. The only questions in my mind, really, were how soon I could start, how high I might rise, and what I
could do to fill my time productively until then.

As it turned out, I followed my mother's path at first. I wasn't
looking to be a model. It just kind of happened. I met an Elite modeling agent when I was about ten years old who told me to call her when
I got older, but I didn't give it a serious thought. I was ten! I had absolutely no interest in modeling. Remember, I was the tomboy who never
could see the point of that whole Barbie doll thing. But then I ran into
the same agent again when I was thirteen or fourteen, and at that point
I started to think there might be something to it. I still wasn't all that
interested in modeling, but I'd developed a taste for fashion and

81

style—and, above all, for making money. Modeling seemed to offer a
way in on all fronts: all the clothes a teenager could possibly wear, all
the exotic locales she could possibly visit, all the money she could possibly spend. When you think about it, there aren't a whole lot of ways
for a serious young teenager to make money, other than babysitting or
the usual summer and minimum-wage jobs. Successful models, on the
other hand, can make a ton—more than I could hope to spend. Even
moderately successful models do okay, and as a kicker I'd get to wear
all these great clothes and see a little bit of the world from a perspective other than my mother's.

I finally decided to pursue a modeling career when I got to Choate
for two reasons. One, I felt a little disconnected at boarding school. I
was a city girl at heart, I guess, and the sleepy pace of Wallingford,
Connecticut was . . . well, a little too sleepy. Modeling seemed like a
good way to fill the space between classes and exams. And two, I'd already given a lot of thought to what it would be like for me to follow
in my father's footsteps in real estate and have to hear that the only
reason I was making it was because of my last name. At fourteen,
the idea of working in a field that had nothing to do with my father
was incredibly appealing. He was fairly ubiquitous—not just in real
estate circles but all across New York's financial community. However, his influence didn't quite reach to the world of fashion, so that
went into the plus column. It would be all on me. Either designers or
photographers would like the way I looked, or they wouldn't. Either
they'd think I'd sell their product or wear their clothes well, or they
wouldn't. No designer was going to put an unattractive girl into his
show because of who her father is—especially a father who has nothing to do with fashion.

My first assignment was a shoot for *Elle* magazine with Gilles
Bensimon, one of the fashion industry's foremost photographers. I
came away thinking, Okay, Ivanka, this could possibly be interesting.
Next, I did a campaign for Tommy Hilfiger, and by then I'd shot
straight past interesting all the way into *keep your guard up* territory.

It was just my second assignment, but already I was realizing that models were the meanest, cattiest, bitchiest girls on the planet. It was like being cast in a cheesy Aaron Spelling show—only with real people, real money, real consequences. The more I kept at it, the more it confirmed my opinion of my new colleagues. For the most part, models were entitled, unsupervised, undereducated, pampered teenagers whose every success came as the direct result of someone else's disappointment. Of course, this applies to almost all of our accomplishments when someone gets overlooked or turned down, but here it seemed so personal. Everyone was so young, so insecure. A lot of the models I knew appeared to relish landing a job over another girl. In fact, the more girls a model could disappoint on her way to the top, the better; that seemed to be the general rule. If I ever wanted to hear what people were saying about me behind my back, all I had to do was step behind the stage at a fashion show or skulk around a dressing room on a shoot and I'd get an earful. And it didn't even have to be behind my back.

But I kept at it. My parents agreed to let me pursue my modeling career aggressively, provided I kept my grades up at school. Their idea of keeping my grades up was basically a 4.0 average, and I guess they set the bar so high thinking it would be a good way to get me to give up modeling, but I held up my end. When I was a little bit older, I had a car at school—one of the concessions to my "job"—and the routine was that I'd drive ninety minutes down to New York for a "go-see" after class and then head right back to Connecticut a few hours later. If a call or a shoot interfered with a class, I'd usually let it go and look ahead to the next one.

There was plenty of work, it turned out. Not just for me but for all models. It was a busy, heady, frantic time in the fashion business. The look back then was Heroin Chic. That was the ideal. Happily, that wasn't *my* look, but I seemed to fit in the ancillary baby-faced category. It was such a stark contrast to the gaunt, strung-out appearance of most models, but it was very much on display. My baby face, chubby cheeks and all, perched on the body of a grown-up. I was very skinny at the time but also very tall, so it was a funny juxtaposition, to see this cherubic face on an adult body, adorned in all these outrageously glamorous and expensive clothes.

OWNING YOUR LOOK

I remember standing on line at a go-see—the castings really were like cattle calls—listening to one frightening girl talk to another frightening girl about how she'd stayed up all night to achieve the stressed, strung-out look that seemed to be called for on this shoot. These girls were a bit older than me, possibly even adults, but it was such a strange, weird, ridiculous conversation. It would have been silly if it hadn't been so deeply disturbing. The Heroin Chic look was bad enough, but here these poor girls were manufacturing that look to get ahead. Starving themselves for it. Staying awake for it.

I listened in and thought, This isn't for me—at least not in the long run.

But I took full advantage of it just the same. Modeling fit neatly into my schedule and provided me with a world of opportunities. I got to travel. Paris, London, Milan, Melbourne . . . On a lot of these trips, I stayed with family friends, but occasionally I'd stay with the other models. This was an odd, sometimes unsettling arrangement. We were very young and often unsupervised, and some of the girls were terrible role models, but I suppose this forced me to be self-reliant and organized and to make good decisions. If my parents had realized how lightly supervised I would be and how little we'd see of our supposed chaperones, they would never have let me go, but it forced me to grow up pretty darn fast.

I'd always been something of an old soul, so this wasn't such a stretch. I learned a lot, just not about modeling. What I needed to know about modeling I picked up right away. The real education came from being around all the wonderfully eccentric designers, brutally honest casting agents, and mother hen–type bookers. On the editorial side, I got to deal with a lot of influential media types; on the runway side, there were event planners and public relations professionals, not to mention the influential jet-setters who crowded into our shows. There are a lot of interesting characters in and around the fashion world, I learned. It's almost a microcosm of the real world, so every assignment offered a short course in getting along with all different types of people, in all different types of situations. Whenever I'd traveled with my parents, I'd tended to follow their leads, but here there was no one to follow, so I was forced to develop my own approach. I learned how to carry myself, how to fit myself in, how to stand apart, and how to adapt to all the different cultural mores and expectations.

The most tangible advantage of my brief modeling career was that I made some money—quite a lot, actually. My parents' idea was to let me keep what I earned, but I never really touched any of it. Whatever I made, I sent right over to Ace Greenberg at Bear Stearns, who handled a lot of our family accounts. I sat down with Ace, the former CEO of Bear Stearns and then chairman, and we talked about a conservative portfolio of investments—one-third in stocks, one-third in bonds, one-third in cash. It's basically the same ratio I keep today, but as a kid I was happy to be guided. Amazingly, my parents didn't really get involved in this aspect of things. They trusted me to make good decisions with the money I earned, and I did. (They trusted Ace, too, I suppose—which might explain why they gave a kid so much rope.) I didn't cash my checks and go crazy, like a lot of the girls I was working with. But from time to time, if I wanted a special something, I'd buy it for myself. Guilt-free.

STEPPING AWAY

Modeling was just a stopgap for me until I was old enough to get a real job, and while I was an undergraduate at Penn, taking courses at Wharton, I started to map out a career strategy. Okay, so maybe there was no map and nothing really resembling a strategy, but I did start to give it some serious thought. It was about time. All along, my plan had been to work for my father, but I hadn't really thought about how or in what capacity. All I knew was that I wanted to be a builder. It was a plan only in the sense that it seemed inevitable. Now there were all these other options to consider. A lot of my friends were contemplating a move to graduate school, but that didn't make a whole lot of sense to me just then. Law school held real appeal—in fact, it still does!—because I thought I could learn a set of skills that would apply to any business setting, but an MBA seemed redundant. For me especially. At Wharton, I was already taking most of my classes with graduate students. An MBA is great if you don't quite know where you're going; it can point you in the right direction or introduce you to invaluable contacts. It's important if you work for a company that requires it for advancement, which is the case at a lot of the major financial institutions. But it didn't really add a whole lot to the résumé I was building.

I went from thinking I had it all figured out to feeling as if I was still very much finding my way. I was fortunate enough to receive some straight-shooting career advice during this period from one of my professors, Peter Linneman. When I got to Wharton, my father told me to take as many classes as I could with the guy. They'd run into each other in many business settings, far removed from the classroom, and my father told me that Professor Linneman knew his stuff.

Trouble was, that was easier said than done. Professor Linneman was one of the most popular professors at Wharton. He's exceptionally bright and thoroughly engaging, but the best thing about him is that he's a real-world pragmatist. He's not one of those academic types who spends his days in an ivy-covered building, analyzing trends and assessing theory. No, he puts his theory into practice, which meant he could offer a real frontline perspective to the material.

When I couldn't get into Professor Linneman's seminar through normal means, I just showed up. Very often, that's a great strategy—

showing up. It's half the battle, right? At least that's the old saying, only I've found that in some cases it's more like three-quarters. Anyway, it's usually a good gambit: show your face, and you're way ahead, because most people are too timid to attempt even this much. They'll take no for an answer and head home. Showing up put me face-to-face with Professor Linneman, which was something, but it couldn't quite get me past the fact that this particular seminar was for graduate students only. That was something else entirely, although I saw it as just a small technicality. As a fallback, I was prepared to simply audit the course for no credit; I'd already made time for it in my schedule and figured I would make myself known to Professor Linneman in such a way that he couldn't help but wave me in to some other seminar the following semester. But I wasn't prepared to give up just yet—and after a few days and a few hurdles I managed to con my way in. There sat I and three or four other undergraduates with the same idea, in a class full of MBA candidates.

I ended up taking a few courses with Professor Linneman. He became a kind of mentor, someone other than my father I could talk to for advice and insight into real estate development and a possible first career move. All along, my focus had been on learning everything I could, as quickly as I could; unlike a lot of my peers, I wasn't too worried about finding a job, I guess because working for my father at Trump and learning the business at his side was the natural next step.

Then, just before the start of my final semester, Professor Linneman called me into his office one afternoon. He wanted to discuss my career plans. I told him that I was planning to work for the Trump Organization after graduation. He suggested that I consider a different tack. He had a number of friends and contacts in real estate circles, he said, particularly on the development side. A lot of them were in the habit of reaching out to him to recommend talented students they might consider hiring. He wanted to know if he could pass my name along, if I would even consider an opportunity outside our family business.

"Frankly, Professor, I'm flattered," I said. "But I don't want to put you in a bad spot by putting me up for a job, because ultimately we both know where I'll wind up. At the end of the day, my goal is to join the family company and work for my father."

"You should think about that, Ivanka," Professor Linneman said. "Working with your father is a tremendous goal, and in the long run it's probably your best bet, but don't be in such a rush. You should think about getting some experience elsewhere before going back to the Trump Organization to make your career there."

Peter Linneman was the kind of guy who didn't mince words. If he was telling me to think about signing on someplace else, that was the very least I could do. If I didn't, I'd be selling myself short. I talked to my dad about it, too. And my brothers. (My older brother, Don, had gone directly to work for my father after graduating from Wharton, so he was uniquely qualified to weigh in on this.) Gradually, I came to realize the value of my professor's advice. He wasn't trying to discourage me from following my dream of working in the Trump Organization or working alongside my father to grow the Trump brand. Not at all. He was simply encouraging me to try on another perspective or two before returning to the fold—if nothing else, to gain a sense of self-worth in a context that had nothing to do with my place in the family. It would be a continuing education of a kind and a chance for me to learn what it's like to work in a more typical business environment and to be yelled at by a boss who wasn't my father.

I already had the nuts and bolts in place. I even had a breadth of entry level–type experience, from a variety of summer jobs and internships. Academically, I felt as if I was ready to take on any assignment—but of course it's one thing to earn straight A's in school and quite another to put that knowledge to work. My biggest worry was that I'd get started on my real estate career and find out I was just okay—good enough and nothing more. It was a terrifying prospect. Mediocrity, to me, was the worst possible outcome. If I went to work for my father and turned out to be ill suited and unprepared, he'd fire me. In a heartbeat. But if I were just barely good enough to keep my job, that would be a whole other worry. Just then, looking ahead to the career I imagined, I didn't think I could continue on in the family business knowing I wasn't contributing mightily, that my father and brothers were carrying me, or that I was neither talented enough to be promoted to the top nor terrible enough to get booted.

So, with some encouragement from Peter Linneman and the enthusiastic endorsement of my father, who immediately saw the wisdom in this approach, I went off on my first real job interview—thinking that if I was meant to be mediocre I'd do well to discover it someplace else, far away from the family business. I met with a team at Forest City Ratner, a diversified real estate development and management company that in many ways mirrored the family business aspects of the Trump Organization. Bruce Ratner knew my father, but only casually. He knew that in all likelihood I would join my father at Trump in a year or two, but he was nevertheless interested in bringing me on. In essence, his team would be renting me instead of hiring me, but that was implicit. In fact, at Forest City Ratner, it's a prerequisite for any member of the Ratner family who wants to join the business to work elsewhere for at least two years before doing so. And it's not enough just to *work* someplace else. Here's one of those cases where merely showing up doesn't quite cut it. The person has to be successful in that endeavor, as well.

To be sure, with this kind of culture already in place, the Ratner group was very nurturing of the fact that I might need a place to test my mettle away from my father, and they were only too happy to give me that opportunity. They couldn't have been more candid or more encouraging, and even though I went in to that job interview with a healthy dose of uncertainty about working anywhere else but the Trump Organization, I left thinking, Hmmm . . .

In the end, Forest City offered me a job and I jumped at it. It was so exciting—a spectacular opportunity, really. The money wasn't great (not by prerecession Wharton standards), but my $50,000 base salary was in line with what my father tended to pay new hires just out of college. Certainly, it was well within the industry norms. Outside of the New York–based real estate development companies, though, the money was actually on the low side. A lot of my friends going into investment banking were leaving Wharton with six-figure salaries, and my annual paycheck wouldn't even touch what I used to make in a single modeling campaign when I was just fifteen or sixteen years old. But I wasn't about to quibble. I didn't want to work for a financial firm, which was where most of my Wharton pals were landing their big-ticket jobs. I wanted to sink or swim in an environment that would closely resemble what I'd find back home, at the Trump Organization—only I was determined to do so on my own terms.

FIGHTING MEDIOCRITY

One final thought on my fears of mediocrity: they were *my* fears. Not everyone is cut the same way. I grew up believing that excellence was expected of me. In school, on the runway, in the way I carried myself around my parents' influential friends. Anything less was unacceptable—to me. To be fair to my parents, this was a pressure I put on myself, except where my grades were concerned. Here they quite reasonably expected the very best, because they knew what I was capable of. But when it came to work and how I moved about in the real world, this type of thinking was mine alone. I suppose my parents grew up with their own version of this self-inflicted need to excel, and my brothers too, which might explain why they're all so successful, but I was self-centered enough back in college to think I'd invented this type of pressure, these kinds of impossible expectations.

Naturally, I recognize that we can't all be great at everything we do—if we could, we'd all be leaders and visionaries—but we can all be great at something. If you're merely surviving at work instead of thriving, perhaps it means you're not in the right field. Or maybe you don't have enough passion for what you're doing to succeed at the highest level. I've worked with people who are much more knowledgeable than I am, who are way more intelligent than I am, with far more experience, but I can usually get the better of them on a deal because of my dogged determination. It's just not possible to have that kind of focus if you're not passionate about what you do. Greatness will forever be just out of reach. If you don't absolutely, thoroughly, completely love, love, love what you do, you'll never have what it takes to make it to the top.

Enthusiasm and drive can certainly compensate for experience, I've discovered. At least, they can fill some of the gaps that come with inexperience. Look at the most successful people in any field. The most famous CEOs. The most talked-about entrepreneurs. The biggest, boldest visionaries. They're the ones who seem to be operating in overdrive, the ones overflowing with enthusiasm. They tend not to be the type of people who move on the strength of their pure genius alone or who lock themselves in their offices and crunch numbers all day. For the most part, successful people manage to graft their intellectual gifts on their personal strengths in such a way that their ability to connect with others is what takes them to the top. Their ability to network and maximize their relationships and use them to advantage— that's key.

FIRST (AND LASTING) IMPRESSIONS

I signed on at Forest City Ratner as part of a thirteen-person development team working on a shopping center project in Yonkers, just north of New York City. We were in the preconstruction stage of the development cycle when I joined, so I was able to hit the ground running along with everyone else. At least, that's what I told myself at the time. In truth, I didn't have the first idea what I was doing, but I caught on soon enough.

One of the appealing aspects of this initial assignment was that I wouldn't be competing directly with any Trump Organization projects. That was important to me at the time, although the primary attraction was that I'd be working with a great group of knowledgeable people on an exciting project—a 1.2-million-square-foot shopping center that would, we hoped, be a core profit center for the company.

My first day didn't exactly get off to a flying start—although it was certainly an *early* start. My big thing when I was younger was to be on time, and it remains an obsession, drilled into me by my parents at a very young age. The message I got at home was to take extra-special care with other people's time. If someone was carving out the time to meet with you or hire you, it was your responsibility to do them the courtesy of being prompt. It was basic. My father used to say there was no such thing as being early to a business meeting. You could be on time or you could be late, and that was it. Don't leave anything to chance, he always told me. No one wants to hear about traffic or a train delay or a lousy sense of direction.

In this regard he really practiced what he preached. Once, when he was married to Marla Maples, we were waiting and waiting at the airport to take off on his private plane for Palm Beach. Marla was always late; it was a big point of contention between them. My father had just about given up on Marla making it to the plane by our scheduled take-off time, and we were getting ready to roll down the runway when I saw Marla's car pull up alongside. The door to the plane was already closed. The engines were roaring. We were good to go. And there on the tarmac was Marla, all frantic and frazzled and running just a little behind.

I tapped my father on the shoulder and told him to look out his window, but when he saw Marla all he did was throw up his hands. He didn't tell the pilot to stop, and we took off anyway.

I said, "Come on, Dad. She's just five minutes late." I knew he'd turned punctuality into an art form, but this seemed a bit excessive even for him.

He said, "No, Ivanka. You have to be on time."

Of course, my father wouldn't have drawn such a firm line if Marla hadn't been chronically late. That was just one time too many, as far as he was concerned. And it was the last time, too, because she never missed the plane again.

Anyway, that's the mind-set I took with me to my first day on the job. I was determined to get off to an early start. It was the Tuesday after Labor Day. I'd come back a day early from a weekend in the Hamptons with some friends, just to get acclimated and organized. My plan was to use that Monday to make a trial run to Brooklyn, where Forest City was based. I wasn't used to taking the subway outside Manhattan, but it was really the only way to get back and forth on a budget and a tight schedule. And I came away thinking it was a good thing I'd set off on that trial run. I got ridiculously lost. I took the wrong train. Then I got off at the wrong stop and had to wait for another train. It was Labor Day, so the trains were running on a holiday schedule, which meant they were few and far between, but when I factored in my commuting time for my first *real* trip to work I didn't want to take any chances.

By Tuesday morning, I thought I had it figured out. I set two different alarms so I wouldn't oversleep. I'd tried on several outfits the night before, so I could be sure to wear the exact right one. I exercised. I ate breakfast—and back then, I *never* ate breakfast. I wanted to make certain I was fully and doubly and completely prepared. Then, thinking back to my disastrous trial run the day before, I left my apartment by six in the morning, wanting to leave enough of a cushion in case of an unusually long commute. Twenty minutes later I had arrived. There wasn't a soul in the office. The lights weren't even on! I ended up sitting in the hallway on the floor by the front door, feeling like an idiot, waiting almost two hours for someone to show up and unlock the door.

Be prepared? Be on time? Yeah, right.

I'd had a horrible anxiety dream the night before, and I kept playing it over and over in my head the whole time I was sitting on the floor outside my new office. I was walking through a construction site with my new boss when one of the construction workers whistled at me. I must have been worrying about this scenario as I drifted off to sleep, and it came back to me in my dreams. It had been a recurring nightmare in the weeks preceding my first day of work, and here it found me one final time. As I sat there outside the corporate entrance waiting to get started on my first job, I put myself back into my dream. The anxiety I'd felt while I was sleeping came rushing back in full force. Of course, that type of thing had happened to me before—many times, actually, on my father's construction sites when I'd worked for him over the summers. But in those cases, the workers never realized I was the boss's daughter when they started hooting and hollering, and it didn't much matter how I responded. Then someone would inform the offending hard hat who I was, and he'd fall all over himself apologizing. I'd laugh it off and act as if it were no big deal. Here, though, the prospect woke me with a start, and I couldn't shake thinking that I needed to come up with a disarming line to defuse the situation and keep the embarrassment level to a minimum. After all, I kept reminding myself, my new boss would be observing my reaction, which meant that if anything like that happened it would put me into an uncomfortable, no-win situation. If I ignored the inappropriate remarks, I might come across as weak. If I responded too harshly, I'd be a tightly wound witch.

Ah, the perils of the young blonde, walking a construction site to the cacophonous catcalls of the big, hairy behemoths on the crew . . .

It was such a cliché—but when you walk onto a construction site as a young woman you understand *why* it's such a cliché. It comes with the territory, but that didn't keep it from being a legitimate worry. I wasn't worried for myself, mind you, because I never felt threatened or intimidated by any of these taunts, but I worried how I'd come across. I wanted to blend in during those first days, so I obsessed.

God knows, I'd certainly given myself a lot of time to think of an appropriate response—and, thankfully, I never left the building that day, so the problem never came up. When it finally did, it was no longer an issue, because I'd developed enough confidence to deflect the whistles with relative ease, and here we bump into an important lesson for any young woman, in any work setting: sexual harassment is never acceptable, and we must stand against it. At the same time, we must recognize that our coworkers come in all shapes, stripes, and sizes. What might be offensive to one person might appear harmless to another. Learn to figure out when a hoot or a holler is indeed a form of harassment and when it's merely a good-natured tease that you can give back in kind. My perspective is a little skewed on this and my experiences a bit extreme, because some of the guys on our crews can be real *guy* guys, but I've gotten pretty good at separating the *real* harassment from the benign behavior that seems to come with the territory. Sometimes it might be tough to tell the difference, I realize, and in that case you should do whatever feels right and comfortable. If you're not sure, confide in a female colleague and get her take. Or, approach the offending party directly, with an uninvolved coworker in tow, and say something like "Look, I know you're just messing around, but it makes me really uncomfortable, so I'd appreciate it if you'd find some other way to amuse yourself."

As I look back on that initial uncertainty, I'm reminded that I made a conscious effort early on in my career to play down the fact that I was an attractive young woman. I don't mean to blow smoke my own way here, but I *had* been a reasonably successful fashion model. Not that it mattered much. Some of these construction guys would whistle at just about anyone, as long as she was chromosomally correct. Yet, because I was looking to avoid confrontation, I was almost afraid to be feminine on the job, which in retrospect was probably a mistake. I worked in a very male environment, not just on the job site but in our offices as well. Real estate development is a male-dominated field, so I concealed my femininity and wore my hair center-parted, pulled back into a bun. I tended to dress ultraconservatively, in plain black pantsuits.

At bottom, there was nothing about my appearance to suggest that I was a confident young woman—which, after all, was what I was aiming for. Now, all these years later, I wish I'd presented myself a little differently, with a little more personality. At some point I realized that I wasn't a stiff or a stick-in-the-mud. I was a fashion-forward kid just out of college, all of twentysomething, ready to make some noise and shake things up. The way I dressed should have reflected who I was and how I approached the job; it should have reflected *me*. Not some whistle-proof persona I thought it was incumbent upon me to project. It would take me a while to gain the confidence I needed to express myself in this way, but it would come—after I got my footing and felt a little more sure of myself at work. Now I have no problem wearing pink to the office and expressing my feminine style in an office-appropriate way! Because I finally realized that I'm never going to fit the part—or anyone's expectations of what I should look like. I can be on a construction site or at a conference table with a bunch of middle-aged bankers and lawyers. Either I can be comfortable with my appearance and see it as an advantage—standing out in a crowd isn't *always* a negative!—or I can be insecure and self-conscious. Now I choose to put it to work *for* me, not *against* me—keeping in mind, of course, that I should always look polished and professional and appropriate.

Once the anxiety and overpreparedness fell away, I was able to focus on the job itself—and here again the Forest City Ratner team were wonderfully patient and accommodating. They allowed all of us new hires to chart our own course and find our way. They even humored us by letting us sit in on discussions and deliberations that were just a little bit beyond our pay grade at that point in our careers. I wanted to be in on the construction meetings. I wanted to attend our predevelopment planning sessions. But I wasn't an architect. I wasn't an engineer. I didn't have a whole lot to offer, but my supervisors seemed inclined to let me figure things out as I went along.

If a young kid right out of college doesn't have training in a specific area, the obvious place to stick him or her is in sales and marketing. If you're a pretty girl with the ability to b.s., so much the better. That's how I spent the bulk of my time in the beginning—selling, selling, selling—and I wasn't crazy about it. I was good at it—hey, I'm a Trump!—but I didn't love it, so I was always carving out time to do something else. Somehow, I convinced one of the architects to teach me how to use AutoCAD, a computer program that allows you to manipulate blueprints. It was like being given the keys to a whole new world.

At some point I looked up and saw that the other new hires who'd signed on at the same time were not advancing at the same rate as I was. I paid attention to this kind of development because that had been one of the reasons I had joined the company to begin with, as a way to measure myself against my peers. No, it wasn't a competition. No, I wasn't looking to outpace or outperform my colleagues in order to get ahead and stay there. We all got along extremely well and rooted for one another to succeed. But I started to notice that I was getting a lot of the more interesting assignments. I was taking on more responsibilities. And that was both gratifying and validating.

In the end, it would mean that I could move on to the Trump Organization knowing I had something to offer beyond my last name. And, just as important, it was something to fall back on. In fact, when I went to give notice at Forest City Ratner, the people there tried to convince me to stay. (They offered me summer Fridays off and a hefty raise!) They'd known all along that I would eventually leave, but they seemed to want to keep me around—and that alone gave me a huge psychological edge before stepping back to work in the family business. After all, it's terrifying to think that you won't be good at something you've spent your entire life dreaming about. Working in real estate development with my father had been such a big part of my dreams for as long as I could remember. But underneath all my hopes and aspirations there'd been a nagging worry that I wouldn't cut it.

That I'd be competent, nothing more. That's why those first successful steps at Forest City Ratner were so important to me. That's why I tracked my successes there, however small or inconsequential they might have seemed to someone else. To me, they were elemental—because now if there were ever any friction with my father, or my brothers, or if things didn't work out for any reason, I would have the confidence to know I could move on and still be successful in the world of real estate. Not just through the connections I might make or the family name I'd still carry, but through the unique skill set and ability I'd bring to the table.

I set my experiences at my first job against the experiences of a lot of my Wharton pals and noticed one compelling difference: most of my friends reported back that what they learned on their first jobs was what they *didn't* want to do for a living. They went off in search of their long-held dreams—in public relations, investment banking, advertising, accounting, whatever. And many came back disappointed, either in themselves or in the careers they'd spent all that time imagining for themselves. That's a great lesson for any young person just starting out: try everything. Intern everywhere. Be bold. Take risks. And recognize as soon as you can if you're heading down the wrong road, because one of the great things about being young is that you can change course relatively easily.

Happily, that didn't happen for me. For whatever reason, my first job only confirmed what I'd known all along—that the life and career I'd dreamed about in development were certainly within reach.

Within me.

TONY HSIEH—CEO, Zappos.com

ON (NOT) NETWORKING

I really dislike business networking events. At almost every one of these events, it seems as if the goal is to walk around and find people to trade business cards with, in the hope of meeting someone who can help you out in business, and in exchange you can help that person out as well.

I generally avoid them, and I rarely carry business cards around with me. Instead, I prefer to focus on building relationships and getting to know people as just people, regardless of their position in the business world. It doesn't even matter if they're in the business world. I believe there's something interesting about anyone and everyone. You just have to figure out what that something is. If anything, I've found that it's more interesting to build relationships with people who are *not* in business because they can almost always offer unique perspectives and insights, and also because those relationships tend to be more genuine.

If you're truly interested in someone you meet, with the goal of building up a friendship instead of trying to get something out of that person, the funny thing is that something almost always happens later down the line that ends up benefiting either you or your business. I don't know why this happens or how, but I've noticed that the benefit from getting to know someone on a personal level usually happens two to three years after you start building the relationship. And it's usually something that you could not possibly have predicted at the beginning of the relationship. Maybe your friend's sister's neighbor was just hired as the VP of a company you've been trying to contact, or maybe someone you met two years ago now has a new tennis partner who'd be the perfect person for that job you've been trying to fill for the past six months.

Zappos.com has been around for over ten years now. We grew from no sales in 1999 to over $1 billion in gross merchandise sales in 2008. When I look back at the major turning points in our history, it seems that most of them were the result of pure luck. Things happened that we could not possibly have predicted, but they were the result of relationships that we had started building two or three years earlier.

So my advice is to stop trying to network in the traditional business sense and instead just try to build up the number and depth of your friendships, where the friendship itself is its own reward. The more diverse your friendships, the more likely you'll derive both personal and business benefits from those relationships later on. You won't know exactly what those benefits will be, but if your friendships are genuine, those benefits will magically appear two or three years down the road.

SIX

RECIPES FOR SUCCESS

You miss one hundred percent of the shots you don't take.

—WAYNE GRETSKY

My experiences coming out of college and entering the workforce were not exactly typical, but they did provide some useful lessons. As a college senior, I remember feeling that I could do no wrong. I was on top of my schoolwork and I had a great setup in a choice apartment. I was finally old enough to go to the best bars in town—and to know the bouncers, thus ensuring entry! Like most of my classmates, I was anxious to get started on the next phase of my life and career, but at the same time I wasn't so sure I wanted this phase to end.

I was firmly committed to the idea of working in the family business, so there wasn't a whole lot for me to think about or worry about as graduation loomed—that is, until my professor sat me down for that all-important career strategy session. Up to that point, I'd just been counting the days until I could begin at the Trump Organization. Yet even though I was wired to work and anxious to get started, I don't think I was entirely ready to give up on being a kid. It was an appealing pause point: my school work was essentially done, my next steps were unfolding in front of me, and I was content to soak it all in. For a lot of us, there's a weird stretch of time between college and career when our head is focused in one area and our feet are planted firmly in another, with our heart torn right down the middle. I wasn't alone in this, and I believe you'll find a similar tug-and-pull in place among today's graduating students. A lot of my Wharton pals had great jobs lined up, but quite a few of them didn't, so there was tension and resentment all around. By the spring of my senior year, I had my Forest City Ratner position all set, but I didn't have it in me to breathe any sighs of relief just yet. There were still all those doubts over whether I'd be up to the job.

RECOGNIZE YOUR PASSION

Then, I got an unexpected phone call. It was early in the morning—about eight o'clock, which to a college student is just about the crack of dawn. I'd been up all night studying for my *final* final exam and had drifted off for an hour or two of much-needed sleep when the phone rang. My first thought was to just let it ring. I didn't feel like talking to anyone just then. I could hardly lift my head off the pillow—it was heavy with sleep and overstuffed with data and insights for my course in advanced real estate investments. But then I realized it might be important, because no one would call a student at eight o'clock in the morning unless it was important.

"Hello," I said, probably sounding groggy and out of it.

"Ivanka, is that you?" said the voice on the other end, a voice I vaguely recognized.

"It is," I said. "Who is this?"

"I'm sorry if I've woken you, Ivanka," the voice said. "It's Anna Wintour. Do you have a few minutes to chat?"

Anna Wintour. The editor of *Vogue*. An icon to millions of women—and quite a few men, too. Someone I'd known for years through my parents—and, later on, through my work as a model. I thought, Why on earth is she calling?

"Of course," I said, trying to shake the tiredness from my voice. "How are you, Anna? It's so nice to hear from you."

Anna explained that she'd heard I was about to graduate but she wasn't calling to offer her congratulations. She was calling to offer me a job. Just like that. She didn't know my plans, but she knew all about my interest in modeling and fashion. "I could only offer you an entry-level position to start," she said, "but if you're serious about fashion it would be a great way to launch your career."

It was an amazing opportunity and an amazing call—a real *pinch me!* sort of moment. Even then, I knew full well I would never have gotten such a fantastic offer if my last name hadn't been Trump, but that didn't make it any less thrilling. Anna Wintour had always been one of my heroes—an intelligent, dynamic, sophisticated woman, a true giant in both fashion and publishing. As an aspiring female entrepreneur, I couldn't imagine a better mentor than Anna. She could teach me a lot, no question. There was even a lesson in the fact that she was reaching out to me with the offer of a job. As an executive, I'd soon learn, you're constantly on the lookout for good young talent. You can't sit and wait for interested applicants to come to you looking for work; you have to go looking for them, and Anna must have seen some potential in me during our previous meetings—so it was flattering and illuminating, all at once.

But I'd already accepted the job at Forest City Ratner, and I wasn't about to give up on my lifelong passion of building a career in real estate. It was nice to be wanted, and I suppose there was a time in my life when it would have been a nice prospect to consider, but it wasn't for me.

"Anna," I said, "I'm so, so grateful for your call and for your generous offer, but I'm afraid I can't accept. I've already agreed to take a job with a real estate development company after I graduate. My plan is to work there for a year or so and then join my father. Real estate is my passion."

I'd bumped into a tough spot: how do you turn down a job without burning a bridge you might need at some later date? I was flattered that Anna Wintour had sought me out in this way, but I didn't want to insult her by rejecting her offer. Granted, it wasn't a job I was looking for and it wasn't a job I particularly wanted at that stage in my fledgling career. Moreover, I couldn't see myself *ever* being in a position where I'd want to switch careers from real estate to fashion. Still, Anna was a good person to have on my side, and I knew enough to treat her offer with respect. So I answered her the only way I could—with complete honesty.

Anna was understanding and graciously wished me luck. She said she'd heard I was leaning toward real estate but thought I might want to give the fashion industry another look. I thanked her again for the call and the thought, we exchanged another few pleasantries, and that was that.

After I hung up, I thought, I didn't see that one coming. Not by a long shot. It was exciting to have someone like Anna Wintour reach out to me about a job. It went straight to my sleepy little head, and I was bursting to tell someone about it. All my friends were asleep, so I called my dad. It was early for me, but it wasn't early for him. He dropped whatever he was doing to take my call.

"You'll never guess who I just got off the phone with," I said, but then I told him before he had a chance to even guess.

When I was finished with my story, he said, "I think you should consider it, Ivanka. Working at *Vogue* sounds very exciting. Anna's the best in the business. You could learn a lot from her."

For a beat or two, I thought maybe I'd dialed the wrong number. I don't know what I'd been expecting, but I certainly wasn't expecting *that*. Frankly, I was shocked that my father would encourage me to pursue a career other than real estate. For years, it was all we'd talked about. For years, I'd done everything I could to make sure I was ready to make a real contribution to the family business when I finally graduated and got the opportunity. For years, it had been a kind of given. His take on this out-of-nowhere, entry-level *Vogue* position took me thoroughly by surprise, and it certainly wasn't a surprise of the good or happy variety. I'd just spent the last two years at Wharton studying finance and real estate. What did my father think I'd been doing all that time? Wasn't he excited at the prospect of me joining his company, even if that prospect was still a few years away? Didn't he think I had what it took to make it as a developer?

I couldn't think how to respond, so I raced off the phone. I still had that *final* final exam coming up later that morning, and I didn't want to get too distracted by all these unanswered questions. There was enough going on in my head already, and I was determined to end my academic career on a strong note. I tried to go back to sleep, but of course I couldn't. I was too shaken by those two phone calls. Too emotional. Too confused. Too everything.

Over the next few weeks, as graduation loomed, my thoughts kept returning to my father's comment. Actually, they went all the way back to when I was at boarding school, making the argument for pursuing a modeling career. It was a way to make my mark outside my father's considerable sphere of influence, in an industry where his name wouldn't open any doors or lead directly to any opportunities. (In the ultimate irony, he ended up buying a modeling agency . . . but that prospect wasn't on the radar back then.) Any successes I managed to find would be totally on me. If I failed, it would be on me, too. That was appealing to me as a kid—and I realized it was still appealing to me as a young adult. Whatever I did next, after school, I wanted to *own* it. To *earn* it. I didn't want anything to be handed to me, and it took hearing what sounded like doubt from my father to get me to question my decision to follow in his footsteps.

At the time, I didn't particularly love the idea of working in fashion, but I was determined to make my way on my own terms, on my own strengths. I went from being completely confident and pumped about my upcoming job to being completely unsure of myself—all on the back of this otherwise positive, affirming phone call from Anna Wintour. To be sure, it wasn't the call itself that left me reeling, it was my father's reaction to it. It was the thought that my ultimate mentor might be trying (not all that subtly!) to tell me to do something else for a living.

One day, just before graduation, I finally brought it up with him again. I wanted to know what the hell he'd been thinking when he said I should consider Anna's offer.

"Please don't doubt my confidence in you, Ivanka," he explained. "I only suggested you think about that job at *Vogue* because I wanted to see how serious you were about going into real estate. I wanted *you* to see for yourself how serious you were about it."

"Of course I'm serious about real estate," I said. "I've been fascinated by it since I was a child. You know that as well as anyone. I've taken every chance you've given me to work at the company. Summer jobs, whatever. I've learned everything I can learn without actually being there and living it firsthand. I've been studying it at school . . ." I would have gone on and on, but my father cut me off.

"I'm aware of everything you've done," he said, "and I'm enormously proud of your accomplishments. I just thought we should both be sure that you weren't doing all these things because you felt that was what was expected of you. If real estate isn't the right fit for you, I wanted you to know it was okay with me."

I thought, Well, *that's* a relief. And it was. Here I'd been thinking my father didn't really believe I had what it took to make it in real estate, and all along he'd just been testing my resolve. Beneath that feeling, though, I realized I was also a little pissed that he'd put me through those doubts and worries, but the feeling of relief won out. And it was a relief for him, too, to hear how passionate I was about wanting to work as a developer. As a boss, he wouldn't want me around if I wasn't dead certain about my path. As a father, he wouldn't want me to move forward on that road for the wrong reasons. He wanted his children to have passion for whatever we chose to do. Real estate was his passion, but it didn't have to be ours. As long as we cared about what we were doing, we'd have the focus and determination to get our bearings and then thrive—in *any* career.

I'd heard my father speak many times about the importance of loving what you do. It was one of the great themes in our house as I was growing up. But now that I was about to graduate from college and take my first real job, his message really hit home. He didn't want to see me spin my wheels in a profession I wasn't passionate about. He believes that when you bring your heart and soul to a job, you can't lose—but when you don't, you'll always lose to someone who does. Bottom line: he believed that if I wasn't prepared to eat, drink, and sleep real estate, I shouldn't enter the field. And it took hearing it from him that one final time, in the context of the unexpected phone call from Anna Wintour, to get me to realize that I believed the very same thing.

STANDING OUT IN A CROWDED FIELD

Just before graduation, many of my classmates worried how to separate themselves from the pack. It was a two-part worry. First, they had to land a job once they got out of school; and second, they had to make an immediate splash once they got the position so that they could get off to a great start and ultimately angle themselves for promotion.

The key to both objectives, I realized then as now, is strong interviewing and interpersonal skills. I can't emphasize this enough. You'll need to call on these skills not only to land a job but to do well once you start working, because the way you carry yourself in meetings, the way you interact with your bosses, the way you collaborate with your new peers will have everything to do with how you're viewed at your place of employment. It's all interviewing, of a kind. It's basic communication. As a (relatively) young woman who now works in upper management, I have a unique, twentysomething perspective on the ways young people go through these particular motions. I'm young enough to remember how tough the interviewing process was for me and for a lot of my friends back in school and fortunate enough to occupy a post where I get to see from a management perspective how recent graduates handle the transition. A lot of candidates don't do such a good job of it, I'm afraid. Now that I'm on the other side of the desk, I've met many applicants who looked impressive on paper but couldn't seem to get out of their own way in an interview. In a competitive business environment where MBAs are fighting over entry-level positions, there's no longer any room to make a poor impression in an interview.

I often find myself sitting across the table from someone very close to my own age. That's a bit unusual, I suppose. I mean, a lot of my friends are still pounding the pavement looking for their dream jobs—actually, in a lousy economy, many of them would settle for *any* job, at least for the short term. Yet here I am, interviewing other freshly minted graduates on the prowl for dream jobs of their own. I understand how daunting the interview process can seem for a young person just starting out (I get an earful of horror stories from my unemployed girlfriends every week!), but as an executive I can't understand why these otherwise qualified candidates don't spend a little extra time on their presentation skills to give themselves the edge they certainly deserve.

A word of advice: your interview is about *you*. It's not about the school you went to, what you majored in, what your GPA was, or who your parents happen to be or know. Most of that stuff is right on your résumé, and it might even have gotten you into the room, but it won't get you much farther. Once you land an interview, you must light it up with your knowledge, confidence, and enthusiasm. With *you*.

INTERVIEWING BASICS

Make an effort to surprise the person across the table—not in a shocking, what-the-hell-is-wrong-with-this-person? sort of way but in a pleasing, gee-that's-a-wonderfully-unexpected-turn! sort of way. Tell that person something he or she might not usually hear and show why you'd be an interesting person to have around the office. Be charming, but be yourself. (That shouldn't be so hard, should it?)

Keep in mind that in addition to evaluating whether you possess the skills and experience needed for the position, interviewers are also assessing whether you are someone they could work with.

Are you agreeable, affable, fun, interesting?

Do you come across as confident, intelligent, capable, curious?

The interview is not just about *whether* you can do the job but *how* you might approach it. At some level, you have to think the *whether* is a foregone conclusion. You wouldn't be having the conversation if you weren't perceived to be qualified. But are you a person this company wants to represent it in a boardroom or in interactions with clients? Will other employees look forward to meeting you in an elevator or by the water cooler? Or will you be a constant drag on their time and energy and patience?

Remember, the person across the table is sizing you up and measuring all these intangibles, so you'd do well to bring the very best aspects of your personality into the room.

Another few words, as long as I'm on it:

Don't be late. This probably falls into the "Duh!" category, but you'd be surprised how many people show up five, ten, even thirty minutes late to a job interview. It's unforgivable, really. I've heard all sorts of excuses, and they're just that—excuses. It goes back to the Labor Day dry run I made to the Forest City Ratner offices in Brooklyn. If your interview is at three in the afternoon and you think it will take you a little over an hour to get to the location, leave at one. Give yourself a cushion. You don't want to be stuck in traffic or sitting on a stalled train fifteen minutes before your interview. If you manage to arrive just under the wire, you'll look frazzled—not the best way to start such an important meeting. A nice fringe benefit to this strategy is that arriving early sends a powerful signal that you're organized and grateful for the opportunity, traits every employer seeks in a young hire. Plus, you can use the extra time to get settled. Use the restroom and make sure your hair is combed and your shirt hasn't come untucked. Text a friend. Take a walk around the block and listen to some mellow music on your iPod. Do whatever you can to steady your nerves without drawing any unwanted attention to yourself from potential coworkers.

Keep your résumé handy. It's not enough to have it in your bag or tucked away in a folder. I not-so-secretly hate it when I ask a candidate for a résumé and then have to wait thirty seconds while he or she rummages around in a bag for it. I always think, Come on, it can't be a surprise to you that I'm asking for your résumé. It's the one certainty in this whole transaction. If you have only five minutes of someone's time, don't waste one-tenth of it on an unnecessary search. If your bag is a mess and you think there's a chance you might have trouble locating your résumé, place it in a separate 9-×-12-inch envelope beforehand—that way, when you're asked, you'll be able to produce the document in a smooth, confident manner. And whatever you do, don't fold your résumé or crinkle it in any way. Long after your interview has concluded, it'll be the one prompt your interviewer has to remind her of your meeting. Make sure it's a crisp, clean, professional-looking copy that nicely supports the positive impression you hoped to make.

Cover your shortcomings. If your hands are clammy, don't shake hands. If you're worried about your breath, don't stand too close—or, even better, suck on a breath mint before you start the meeting. If you tend to stammer when you get nervous and can't think what to say, write out a few simple declarative sentences about your goals or experiences and commit them to memory. Some people are natural interviewees, while others are overwhelmed and intimidated. If you fall into the latter group, find some ways to bolster your confidence *before* the interview. Once you get going, it's difficult to regroup from an awkward start. One good way to do this is to actually stage a mock interview with one of your friends, to help you get comfortable. It might seem goofy, but it's just another version of the trial run I wrote about earlier. Also, tell yourself that the person interviewing you was not up at two the night before worrying about this meeting. She didn't leave early to make sure she would be on time. She probably wasn't even thinking about the interview at all until a few minutes before it started. At the same time, remember that she is interested in what you have to say, and concluding that you are indeed the perfect candidate for the job would certainly make her life at work a little easier. Knowing these things should help you to relax and keep the interview in perspective. You might have all the potential in the world, but if you're unable to communicate your abilities confidently and coherently in the alloted time, you won't give the interviewer a reason to hire you.

Dress the part. What you wear will have "first impression" written all over it, so choose wisely and sell the image you want. Personally, I think less of a candidate when he or she is dressed too casually. An interview is a formal process, so dress accordingly. Guys must understand that unless they are applying for a job in professional sports, they should not wear sneakers. For women, it's a mistake to wear flip-flops, tank tops, or short skirts. It doesn't matter how hot it is outside; those pieces are never part of an appropriate interview ensemble. Like it or not, your physical appearance will say an awful lot about you—and you don't want it to say anything awful.

Some guidelines:

- For women, I'd recommend a nice dress or suit, with heels or fancy flats. Basic black is always appropriate. Stay away from short hemlines and exposed cleavage. Also, make sure your hair is presentable (no sloppy ponytails!) but not too done up. Any makeup should be light and professional.
- For men, be clean-shaven and well groomed. Wear a suit. A classic charcoal gray, navy blue, or black suit is always a smart choice. Don't try to stand out with noisy pinstripes or wonky colors. Your goal should be to appear subtle and sophisticated, not loud or flashy. In the it-goes-without-saying department, make sure there are no holes in your socks, buttons missing from your shirt, or anything to suggest an unkempt, unpressed appearance. And leave your jewelry at home, other than watches or wedding bands.
- For men *and* women, your outfit should be appropriate to the setting. Traditional business environments, such as financial institutions, law firms, government agencies, and Fortune 500 companies, call for traditional business attire. But if you're interviewing at a public relations firm with a client roster made up of rappers and artists, a sports jacket and a skinny tie might be more fitting. Lean toward formal. You might feel uncomfortable wearing a suit while you're being interviewed by some guy in jeans and sneakers, but at least he'll know that you're serious about the job.

Turn your nose "off." Another "Duh!" piece of advice, as long as we're paying attention to looks, but candidates need to think about *every* aspect of their appearance, including their fragrance. I never like it when someone comes into my office smelling like the perfume aisle at the department store. Smell is subjective, and you don't want your perfume or cologne to overwhelm the person across the table. Avoid it. This caution runs to ambient smells as well. Our offices are in midtown Manhattan, and I can't tell you how many times a candidate has come into my office reeking of hot dogs, kebobs, onions, or any of the other grease-inspired smells of New York City street vendors. Steer clear.

Do your homework. Learn everything you can about the company *before* you sit down for your interview. Know its history, its mission, and its competitors, as well as the names of its CEO and top executives. Be able to recognize the company's top products, services, and accomplishments, as well as its disappointments and missteps. If it's a publicly held company, know where its stock closed the night before your interview. Here again, there are no excuses for being ill prepared. These days, almost every company has a Web site, and a Google search will turn up dozens of articles about the business. Read them. Learn how the company is structured, so you can talk knowledgeably about where you might fit into the corporate structure.

Have your answers ready. There are several questions that are asked in the majority of interviews. By preparing for these questions in advance, you will be able to provide the answers that best reflect you, rather than grabbing at the first thing that pops into your mind.

- What skills can you bring to this organization?
- What inspires you about this field/profession?
- What are your short-term and long-term aspirations?
- Can you share a time when you were confronted with a personal or professional crisis and how you handled it?
- What was the last book you read?
- What newspapers or magazines do you read? What Web sites do you visit frequently?

- What kinds of things do you like to do when you're not working?
- Can you give an example of a time when you assumed a leadership role?

Have your questions ready, too. Just before the end of your meeting, you'll be asked if you have any questions about the job or the company. Count on this. It comes up at the end of virtually every job interview, yet I'm stunned by the number of times I've gotten a feeble response like "No, I can't think of anything." I almost always scratch that person off my list immediately, because I can't imagine how a person would let such a no-brainer opportunity slip away. They know the question is coming, right? That's why I tell people to be armed with at least one thoughtful question going into each interview, even if she or he already knows the answer. The question doesn't have to be too complex or revealing, but it should demonstrate that you have a basic understanding of the dynamics of the firm. That said, be sure to avoid asking questions relating to the company's retirement plan, vacation policy, or dress code. Asking about these things in a preliminary interview will make it appear that you're more interested in the benefits than the job itself. Wait until you get the job to pursue this line.

Some additional pointers:

- Decline any offers for tea or coffee before your interview. You don't want to be juggling hot liquid, a purse, and a résumé when your prospective boss reaches out to shake your hand. (Plus, if you drink too much coffee, you might have to suffer through the interview in discomfort, or excuse yourself midmeeting to use the restroom—not the best move if you can avoid it.)

- Leave your coat and any excess baggage with the receptionist, if possible. Carrying all that stuff with you into the meeting will make you appear disorganized.

- Avoid using qualifiers such as *like, maybe, you know* . . . and *ugh!* They tend to make employers cringe. (At least, they tend to make *me* cringe.)

- Don't make the interviewer do all the work. Ideally, I like it when a candidate does about 80 percent of the talking to my 20 percent. If I have to carry any more of the conversation, I start to think I'll always have to be drawing information out of this person.

- Be mindful of the interviewer's time. Even if things are going well, don't overstay your welcome by continuing to chat. Of course, you don't want to keep looking at your watch or putting it out that you have someplace else to be, but you can often get a good read on this with a simple statement such as "You must be terribly busy. I don't want to take up too much of your afternoon."

- Be sure to thank your interviewer for the opportunity, whether or not the meeting went well. And remember, a follow-up thank-you note is always appropriate.

Make a good final impression. If you ace your interview and you're offered the job on the spot (yes, it happens!), don't feel pressured to give an answer right away. It's okay to sleep on it. Some people worry that saying that they need time to consider an offer will signal a lack of conviction. But as an employer, when someone tells me he needs to think about an offer, it makes me think he has other options. If I'm really impressed with the candidate, I might even improve my proposal if I'm told that the uncertainty has something to do with a competing offer by another firm. If this is indeed the case, be sure to say so—and to express your excitement and appreciation. Promise to get back quickly with an answer. What I would not recommend, however, is asking for time to consult with your spouse. I'm sorry, but in my book that's a weak answer. Unless you're talking about a job that will require you to relocate and uproot your family, don't let it appear that you're putting the decision on someone else. If you just want some time to think about it, just say so. But never give the impression that you don't make your own decisions.

FINDING A FIT

I was lucky when I graduated from college, enormously so. I had a clear idea of what I wanted to do and how to accomplish it. I also had an edge: there's no denying that my family name, first-class education, and top-tier contacts gave me a bit of a leg up—a "Trump" card, if you will—but I'm also a firm believer in making your own luck and making the most of your opportunities. Remember, that card will get you somewhere only if you play it to your advantage.

These days, I know a lot of newly minted college graduates and recently unemployed young professionals who feel compelled to go out on as many job interviews as possible, even for jobs outside their areas of expertise. (This can sometimes work, provided the jobs are within an area of *interest*—because if you don't quite know what you're doing *and* you don't quite love what you're doing, you won't get very far.) In any case, they're doing what they can to make their own luck or maybe to turn a string of misfortunes in a more positive direction. I applaud their initiative. After all, if you need a job, you're smart to go where they're hiring. However, if you're looking for a position that might not seem like an obvious fit, it's up to you to explain how you can match your skills to the job at hand. Don't expect the interviewer to make the connection or the extra effort.

Most of us never get to be on the receiving end of the kind of call

I received from Anna Wintour back in college. There, the tables were turned a little. Anna was asking me to consider a position that was a bit outside my wheelhouse, so I didn't have to sell myself or make her see how I might adapt to a new situation. She was coming to me because she already believed in my abilities. But that's not how it usually goes, and it's unrealistic to expect an unlikely job to come looking for you. It might happen from time to time, but you can't expect *time to time* to come around on your calendar when you really need it to.

For the most part, it'll fall to you to go looking for that unlikely job—which just might turn out to be the career you were meant to have all along. But you'll never know it unless you're able to build a persuasive argument in favor of your being hired. That takes some doing. Over the years, I've had several opportunities to interview candidates who had been highly recommended by trusted friends and associates, who nevertheless turned up at my office with no set of qualifications matched to the position I was trying to fill. I see it more and more as the job market tightens and so many experienced people are out of work. But I take this as a positive, as far as management is concerned—an opportunity to discover a wellspring of talent from outside the usual real estate development circles. It's not a deal breaker for me if a candidate hasn't worked in real estate, because I believe in hiring people with diverse professional backgrounds and giving them a chance to prove themselves. What will sink a candidate's chances, however, is when she doesn't make any effort to create a bridge between what she's done and how that experience might benefit the Trump Organization. If she leaves it up to me to connect the dots for her, she's a nonstarter.

I once interviewed a candidate with a strong background in telecommunications. A friend I respected had called to recommend that I meet with this person about an opening. The candidate was extremely articulate and had worked on some important projects at his old firm. His résumé was impressive. Yet as we spoke, I couldn't figure out why he was applying for a job with the Trump Organization. Our core business didn't seem to match any of his experiences or his interests. I'd known as much going into our meeting, of course, but I'd thought our conversation might give this guy a chance to connect some of the dots for me and illustrate a real passion and zeal for the work being done at my company.

I finally said, "I don't doubt you're a highly intelligent, highly capable person, but how do you see yourself fitting in here?"

"Well," the candidate said, "what I'm looking for is a new opportunity more than anything else."

It might have been an honest answer, but it was vague and open-ended. And it certainly didn't do the trick. I heard the candidate's response as a lack of vision, an inability or unwillingness to articulate how his particular areas of expertise or aspects of character might turn out to be assets for our company. It signaled that he hadn't taken the time to research the opportunities at the Trump Organization and indicated a general laziness on his part. Basically, he just wanted a job— *any* job—and ultimately the negative impression he made with that one answer outweighed all the positive ones he had made up to that point. In the end, I had to tell him that I couldn't see the correlation between his interests and the kind of work we were doing.

The lesson here is that it's okay to be bold and brave and turn your goals in an entirely new direction, but you can't simply hang out your shingle and announce that you're available and want to be hired. That kind of strategy especially doesn't cut it in a contracting job market. You have to be willing to adapt, learn, grow—and you have to demonstrate that willingness at every turn. Be bold, but be flexible. Be brave, but not in a reckless or cavalier way. And reimagine your career goals if you must, or even if you wish, but do so proactively, not reactively. Acknowledge that it might be a risk to hire you, if you have no relevant experience, but suggest how your background can be retrofitted in such a way as to accommodate a change of scenery. And promise that you'll work harder than anybody else if given the chance.

I find it so refreshing when I meet potential new hires and hear them talk about where and how they see themselves fitting in at the Trump Organization. It might not be how *I* see them fitting in, but I like that they've taken the time to recognize a path and that they've seen something about our organization that inspires them

One of the best pieces of advice I ever received about pursuing my professional opportunities was just to relax. Chill. Don't go rushing after your career, because you might look up one day and realize you've been going through the motions on a misplaced passion. Your post-college years should be an exploratory time in your professional life. From your early twenties and on into your early thirties, you should feel free to explore your professional prospects. Keep an open mind, and don't expect to get everything right straight out of the gate. Be prepared to start over once or twice. Learn to find excitement in the new opportunities that present themselves instead of bemoaning the things that didn't quite work out for you on your previous course.

Ask yourself if you're in the right job and in the right field. And don't just ask once and set off on a blindly focused journey. Revisit the question even if things are going great. When you're starting out, the right job is the one that's going to teach you the most over the next few years, the one that will expose you to the best, most creative visionaries in your field. If it happens to pay well and offer great opportunities for advancement, so much the better. But you might find yourself considering a low-paying gig with a glass ceiling if it meets some of your other requirements for personal growth and development. For most young professionals, the focus should be on positioning. You want your first job to set up your next one.

Keep in mind, there are no black-and-white answers here. A lot of these issues and concerns will present themselves in shades of gray. It'll be obvious to you when a job or career path isn't working out, just as it will be obvious when you find yourself in exactly the right place. It's that great gray middle zone that will give you the most trouble, in terms of both identifying your dilemma and figuring a way out of it. You don't want to be punching the clock on a career you don't love, at least not while you're young enough to do something about it. The idea is to put yourself into a position to learn as much as you can, as quickly as you can, and to be nimble enough to regroup.

There's an oft-quoted line that's seeped into the culture over the past few generations: "Focus on the journey, not the destination." It comes from an author named Greg Anderson, the founder of the American Wellness Project, and I hear versions of this sentiment all the time. I even found it in a fortune cookie—but I'm afraid there are some pieces missing in this message for aspiring young entrepreneurs. In business, I believe that if you focus *only* on the journey, you'll miss the whole point of the enterprise. There has to be a goal, an end game of some kind; otherwise you're just spinning your wheels. Yes, the journey is important, but the destination is important, too. For my money, it's where you're going *and* how you plan to get there that count. And if you're able to fit yourself in along the way, you'll have things covered on both ends.

B U L L E T I N S   F R O M   M Y   B L A C K B E R R Y

CHRIS DEWOLFE—Co-founder, co-creator, and former CEO, MySpace

ON TEAMWORK AND INNOVATION

One of the keys to success is to work with people who complement your strengths and weaknesses, and one another's. It doesn't matter if it's a for-profit business, a nonprofit, or any other endeavor, this applies across the board. You want to make sure your core values are shared around the table. If your team is working in different directions, analysis, paralysis or infighting can overshadow productivity.

At MySpace, we experienced some early turnover because not everyone shared the same core values or the mission of what we were trying to accomplish. It's easy to talk about values, but they become real only when they're written down and everyone on the team internalizes them. So that's what we did, and these were the qualities and values we wanted everyone on our team to share:

1. Competitive; passionate about the product or mission
2. Exceptionally smart, creative thinkers
3. Nonbureaucratic, nonpolitical—just results-oriented
4. Open-minded and collaborative
5. Big thinkers striving to make a big impact
6. Aggressive movers with the ability to change direction when things aren't working
7. Unwilling to accept mediocrity
8. Deeply curious with a desire to evolve and challenge tradition

Now, these eight attributes might not be right for every company, but identifying them in this specific way and socializing them throughout our organization led to a collaborative, fast-moving atmosphere and allowed us to keep our focus where it needed to be—on providing a better product or service. It allowed us to create an environment for taking risks, and it's been my experience that all successful inventions or projects are a result of taking risks somewhere along the line. Of course, any risky decision needs to be carefully considered and have buy-in from the team. You need to make sure you're all headed in the right direction when you reach that inevitable fork in the road where one decision can drastically change the course of your effort. It's crucial that you foster an environment that includes everyone in the ideation process and doesn't punish an individual for an idea or strategy that fails. The person who generated the idea should be rewarded for creative thinking—never punished. Taking it a step further, he or she should be congratulated publicly by all team members. Send out an e-mail to the whole company, giving kudos to the individual who championed the idea. Even if things don't quite work out the way you envisioned. This reinforces the value of taking measured risks—which at the end of the day leads to innovation and growth.

In the early years, we began expanding into other countries with the goal of adding "a few countries" a year. After eighteen months, we had sites in thirteen different countries. International users now account for 45 percent of users who visit MySpace. It's one of the fastest-growing divisions of our organization. Yet if the international team hadn't aggressively lobbied for this investment, MySpace would have missed the boat outside the United States.

Listen to your core customer, not supposed experts. Your customer is the only one who can tell you the right product or service to offer. What's the best way to connect with your customer? Organize a focus group, and just ask. Or seek out a group of friends and collect their opinions, or check out what people are saying on message boards and forums. Set up a feedback loop with your customers, some way for them to leave comments on your Web site or for you to study traffic patterns on your site or in your store. Where are people going? Who are they? What are they doing? What are they buying? Do they come back? If not, why not? Gather as much insight as you can.

In the beginning, we had a massive number of e-mails and posts from independent bands seeking a home to expose their music to the masses and be discovered. They were frustrated that there was no central place online to connect with potential fans on an intimate basis. MySpace was originally launched as a social network for people to connect with one another around shared interests. This mission would not obviously suggest investing in a hub for musicians, but after taking in all the feedback we realized that music is a key shared interest. It took hearing from all those frustrated bands for us to get that what they were looking for really did fit into our core vision. So instead of kicking the bands off the site as many of our competitors did, we saw an opportunity. Consequently, we decided to invest heavily in MySpace Music, which became a new business for us and the largest music site on the Internet. It also helped to revolutionize the music business and provided an important platform for independent artists such as Lily Allen and Sean Kingston to create a fan base and eventually become major stars. As a heavy-duty side benefit, it exposed more than 130 million MySpace users to music they might never have discovered on their own.

The lesson here is that your original vision might make sense starting out, but it can often be taken in more creative and expansive directions. Take measured risks, and your customers will ultimately lead you to the right decision.

SEVEN

MAKING AN IMPACT

The difference between stupidity and genius is that genius
has its limits.

—ALBERT EINSTEIN

I was only twenty-four years old, barely a year out of college, when I
joined the Trump Organization as the Vice President of Real Estate
Development and Acquisitions. It was an exhilarating moment, one
I'd been looking forward to most of my life—almost from the time
one of the guys on my father's construction crew showed me how to
work the manual levels on a bulldozer when I was about six years old.

There was something about being on a construction site, something about working toward a tangible, *buildable* goal that held enormous appeal. The passion for building was in my bones. I felt myself
pulled toward it again and again throughout my childhood. My friends
used to joke that instead of daydreaming about boys and clothes, I
used to look wistfully into the distance, thinking about tax abatements
and floor plans.

Another indelible, formative memory: when I was about fifteen,
I rode in the cab of a crane being used to build the final floors of the
Trump World Tower—at the time the tallest residential building in

the world, a title it recently gave up to our own Trump Chicago project. That I had made it up to the cab at all was something. The only way to reach it was to take a hoist to the building's eighty-seventh floor—and then, in the open air, climb a ladder the rest of the way. It took several minutes to make the climb, with the wind whipping at me the whole way, but I was determined. I was so excited when I finally reached the cab that I stayed there for more than an hour, taking pictures of the deck below and the Manhattan skyline all around.

DREAM BIG

It was a thrilling view—only my father didn't exactly share my excitement when I told him about it afterward. He wasn't at the site that day, and he wasn't too happy with me for convincing the foreman to take me up. It was so completely dangerous, but I didn't care. I suppose it also bugged him that it was so completely unproductive, because the foreman and the crane operator couldn't do much real work during my sightseeing tour, but as far as I was concerned, it was definitely time well spent, because it was one of the moments that made real estate so important to me, so romantic, so vital. Even now, all these years later, stepping onto a construction site carries a certain, special thrill. It's so gratifying, so validating, to work a project from the ground up—from zoning to financing, from bidding to construction. And then to finally see your efforts materialize before your eyes ... I can't think of another career where the fruits of your labor are so visibly and powerfully on display.

I said as much, in a very public way, in an interview with Barbara Walters. I was still in boarding school and just starting to find work as a model, so I was somewhat comfortable in front of the camera. During the interview, I spoke at length about my desire to follow in my father's footsteps. Then, in all seriousness, I said that I planned to be one of the most successful developers in New York City by the time I was thirty! Can you imagine? Thirty years old! It was a fairly brash, over-the-top thing for a teenager to say, but Barbara didn't call me out on it—at least, not on the air.

Fast-forward several years and now here I was, about to realize my long-held dream. Be careful what you wish for, right? You just might get it. In my case, my new job came with all sorts of pressures, both real and imagined. Some of those pressures were subtle and some decidedly less so. Mostly I felt a tremendous weight to prove to anyone who might have been paying attention that I could handle the responsibilities of such a senior position at such a young age. I tried to learn everything I could about our portfolio and partners and pending deals. For the most part, I had that all covered, but at twenty-four, I was too green to realize that every organization has its own distinct culture, its own rules and way of doing things, its own brand of office politics. If I thought about any of that stuff when I was back in college, I probably just assumed that we'd all do our work and go about our business and our interactions would be fairly clear cut. But that's not how things go in *any* office—and in my case the complex working relationships that sometimes developed were further complicated by the fact that I was the boss's daughter.

My father had set things up in such a way that I was free to make my own mistakes, to succeed or fail on my own terms, to make my own way. He wasn't about to hold my hand or walk me through my first difficult paces. That's not his style, and it would not be mine. That said, he was certainly available to me, and so was the rest of his executive team. I'd grown up surrounded by a lot of those people, so of course they would have been open to sharing their experience and insights, but for some reason I held back. I guess I was a little too timid to take full advantage of the resources they had to offer, so I probably made some mistakes that could easily have been avoided.

My first tentative steps were complicated somewhat by the weight of expectations—or, at least, what I *perceived* as such. Certainly, my father expected a great deal from me, just as I expected a lot from myself. But the expectations of others kind of threw me, because I couldn't safely assume that all of my new colleagues were cheering me on or wishing me well. Some of them were, I'm sure, just as some of them were probably expecting me to fail. I was just a kid, with barely more than a year of experience, and now several key members of my father's organization were reporting to me—so there was every reason to doubt myself.

To be fair, I never felt any resentment directed toward me during that transitional period, but I'm sure there was plenty of ill will bubbling just below the surface. There had to be, right? I mean, I know *I'd* probably have resented it if some kid had swept in and landed a job over me, so I felt extra pressure to prove myself. To prove my worth. Right away. The only trouble with that approach was that it left me feeling that I couldn't ask too many questions without exposing my inexperience. Big mistake. In fact, my determination to figure out everything on my own was like putting my immaturity on full display, because every successful businessperson needs to feel confident enough to ask questions. The most successful people I know spend more time asking questions of the people around them than they do answering them. When you ask a question, you gain another point of view to couple with your own; ask it several times, and you gain even more perspective and put yourself in a better position to make a knowledgeable decision—that's how it works. The learning curve is steep enough without trying to slog up the hill unassisted—and I should have known better. By not taking advantage of the invaluable human resources working in the same company, I did myself and the organization a disservice—all because I was too proud, too shy, too embarrassed to be seen asking for help.

Thankfully, I was able to set things right in that department before too long, and the small mistakes I made by not seeking help were for the most part inconsequential—but that's how you learn, right? You mess up, even in a small way, you make doubly sure not to mess up in that way again. Today, when I have difficulty interpreting a complex legal contract, financial model, or blueprint, I don't hesitate to find someone in the office to explain it to me—and if I can't find someone in-house, I'll reach out to friends and contacts in the field until I can find the help I need to fill in the blanks. There was a time in my career, early on, when I thought it was a sign of weakness if I asked questions, but I've come to believe that that's really a sign of strength. The worst thing you can do when you're not sure of a certain path or approach is to fly blind and hope everything will work out; the best is to seek the help and advice needed to make informed and calculated decisions.

STAY OPEN

The more I work, the more I learn, the more I realize how much I still don't know. It's a humbling thought, but I find great motivation in it. I'd always had a thirst for knowledge, but when I was in school I was content to learn whatever I needed to know in order to meet and master the task at hand and get a good grade. It was only when I started working that I learned to quench that thirst in a more general, all-encompassing way. During my first few weeks at Forest City Ratner, for example, I was determined to learn as much as I could about the construction side of the shopping center project I was working on so that I might make a real contribution in this area—but clearly my skills and knowledge weren't at the same level as those of my more experienced coworkers. So what did I do? I enrolled in night classes in structural engineering and construction at New York University. I wasn't out to get an engineering degree or earn a certificate to improve my standing at Forest City; I was just looking to fill in some of the blanks in my experience. I knew that in order to be a contributing member of the team and to really get the most out of my time at Forest City, I needed to increase my fluency in the language and skills of construction, so I set about doing so.

Over the years, I've continued to take classes at various New York

City institutions, even if they don't directly relate to my responsibilities at Trump. I might audit an art history course—it was my minor at Penn!—or I might enroll in a language class if I think it might help me converse more comfortably with my South American partners. It's tough to fit some of these classes into my crazy-hectic schedule, but I make the extra effort. It's a value-added proposition. Some nights I make it to my class, and some nights I don't—and when I don't, I try not to beat myself up over it. I'll miss a class only for a good reason, such as an important dinner meeting or because I'm finalizing a deal. (For the record, being worn out or too tired or just not feeling like it don't rate as good reasons—for the most part!) Again, I'm not looking to earn a degree but to increase my knowledge base and stimulate my mind. I'm attending for *me*—and if I can't make it one night, I'll make an extra effort to get to the next one.

It goes back to that all-important foundation I wrote about earlier. Just as we search for the best location and the finest materials and develop the most innovative design before breaking ground on a new project, I look to stand on the strongest possible foundation as an individual. Taking courses at night or on the weekends is just one way to keep your skills sharp and gain an edge on your competition. And forget the competition; you'll be lifting yourself up and helping your colleagues by making yourself a stronger, more dynamic member of your team at work.

A lot of my friends go home after a tough day at work and crash in front of the television. Or they'll meet for drinks or a late dinner. Why not dedicate one night each week to continuing your education? Even if it only means making good on that promise you made to yourself to learn how to cook or play the piano? Wherever you live, there's bound to be a viable, valuable program of courses available to you. And if you can't commit to a set night over a full semester, you can likely pick and choose from a wide slate of one-shot lectures, seminars, and readings. One of the great side benefits of taking continuing education classes, I quickly learned, is that it's fairly stress-free. If you were one of those students who pulled out her hair over a midterm exam or a particularly hefty reading assignment, you might find that when you take a class purely for your own benefit it's a whole lot less stressful and more rewarding. The material can speak to you in a whole new way.

One tip: be sure to let them know what you're up to at work, especially if your course or seminar is directly related to your job. Your company might have a program in place to underwrite part of your tuition costs—but even if it doesn't, your boss will be impressed that you're taking the time and initiative to broaden your knowledge base. (Yes, you're doing this for *you*, but if you can score points on the back of it, so much the better.)

Classes aren't the only way to broaden your horizons. The easiest, most cost-effective way to keep abreast of the trends and developments shaping your world is to read as many newspapers and magazines as you can. If you're not in the habit, try it. And keep in mind, when I suggest you read the newspaper, I mean *really* read the newspaper. In depth. Don't just skim past a couple of headlines. Take it all in. Spend some time with the morning newspapers—online, if you like. Go ahead and read Page Six, if that's your thing. (Confession: *I* do!) Check out the sports section or the arts and entertainment pages, but get into the habit of reading the international news, the national news, the editorial and opinion pages. Learn what you can about events in your own community. Above all, spend time in the business section and learn who the players are in your fields of interest—and what deals are in play. Feel free to make your own choices and to read the newspapers and magazines that resonate in your area of interest, but find time to include some of the most respected national newspapers on your reading list, such as *The New York Times, The Wall Street Journal,* and *The Washington Post.* If you're looking for longer, more substantive articles on a variety of issues, check out *The New York Observer, The Atlantic, The Economist,* or *Barron's.* Believe me, there's no shortage of publications that can provide the in-depth analysis and insight you'll need to enrich your skill set at work.

When I was away at boarding school, my father used to cut out articles from the real estate section of *The New York Observer* and send them to me with little notes attached. "What do you think?" he'd write. Or "Interesting article." It was a great way to keep close and connected, but he also wanted to get me thinking about what was going on in the world and to consider how various developments might resonate on a personal level. I do the same thing today with my parents, my brothers, my colleagues at work. If I come across an interesting article, I'll cut it out and send it around the office. (In this way, I guess, I'm entirely old school—I tend to distribute old-fashioned hard copies, torn right from the morning paper.) I encourage my employees to do the same. If they read something of interest or something that relates to one of our projects, they circulate the story, and in this way we get a dialogue going and help keep one another informed in an exchange-of-information cycle. And we encourage one another to read, to think, to learn.

That sense of being embarrassed to ask for help or guidance in an office environment? I got over it in a hurry—once I realized that nobody arrives in her career fully formed, knowing everything there is to know.

ADAPT, CHANGE, GROW

One of the more interesting dynamics in a vibrant, competitive workplace is the tendency of younger employees to want to change their older, more established colleagues. We get frustrated and want to shake things up right away. I call those types "grenade throwers," and I was one myself, for a time, when I was starting out at Trump, but it was a misplaced notion on my part—one that had more to do with arrogance and ignorance than anything else. In the beginning, when I noticed some company veteran going about an assignment in a way I didn't agree with, my first impulse was to think that he was doing something wrong. It took me a while to learn to respect other people's methods and habits.

As a manager, suddenly having authority over older, more established colleagues, my instinct was to try to change their approach and style to suit my own. Another big mistake. Again, it took a while, but I eventually learned that the better approach was to change the way *I* worked with *them*. I tried to be more flexible and to accept the fact that some of them had been at it a long time and knew what they were doing. Their style might not have suited me—but considering the amount of time they had logged at the Trump Organization, an intensely competitive environment, they were probably doing something right. I had to realize that there's no such thing as style over substance in an office setting; we all go about our tasks in a variety of different ways, but being effective and getting things done are what counts in the end.

One of my rookie missteps in this regard came with my misguided attempt to challenge our firm's fashion culture—a silly example, perhaps, but it illustrates the point. Remember, I was still very much a kid when I signed on at Trump, and there were times when a pair of jeans might have better suited my mood than the business occasion. My brothers and I pointed out to my father that a great many firms had instituted some type of "dress-down" or casual day, when employees were encouraged to come to work in slightly less formal attire. It was such a common practice that terms such as "casual Friday" to describe the day of the week that was most frequently set aside for an informal dress code, and "business casual," to describe the style of clothing that emerged on the back of all of this informality, had seeped into the culture.

As more and more business was conducted electronically or over the phone, some firms moved away from a dress code entirely, but my father wouldn't hear of any such thing. His argument against the change made perfect sense. He explained that when the economy is strong and the business environment is generally healthy, people come to his office even for important meetings dressed informally—khakis, open collars, loafers. When times get tough and the environment becomes a little more challenging, those very same bankers and entrepreneurs walk into his office in conservative business attire—polished shoes, silk ties, navy suits. The explanation? According to my father, it's because there's a level of respect and power associated with how we dress. When the high-level executives are doing well, they don't feel the need to prove anything by their appearance. They believe they have the upper hand in discussions, so they dress accordingly. When they're struggling and *hand*—as George Costanza used to say on *Seinfeld*—appears to shift across the table, they look to make every positive impression they can.

My father's position was that we shouldn't wait for a more difficult business climate to show respect—or to expect it in return.

Clearly, he'd spent some time thinking about this. Clearly, my brothers and I weren't the first people on his team to advocate the change. Eventually, we left it alone, because we saw the wisdom in my father's theory. As ambassadors of our brand, we don't want to meet potential partners and project the wrong message of what the Trump Organization stands for, so we err on the side of caution and dress conservatively. You never know how your appearance will be perceived in another corporate culture. What's okay in your firm might not be okay in another one. If you're looking for something from someone else—especially money!—you'll do well to dress to their standards, and since you can't always know what those standards will be, it's best to set your own bar high.

Change is a wonderful and necessary aspect of business, but as I learned with this silly jeans story, sometimes things stay the same for a reason. There were of course many more substantive changes my brothers and I looked to bring about at Trump, including efforts to make better, more meaningful use of database management tools, and finding ways to integrate social media forums like Twitter, Facebook, and MySpace into our corporate culture. We were also instrumental in the redesign of our Web site, and in cementing our company's physical brand and operating standards, as well as hiring younger, hungrier employees to bring new life and a youthful perspective to our organization.

The takeaway for me as I tried to mold myself to the Trump way of doing business was that some things work and should not be changed, but others are in desperate need of a shake-up. The trick comes in knowing which new ideas to pursue, and which to leave alone . . . for the time being.

Another important lesson I learned early on was how important it was to take on difficult assignments. If you are a college student, or even a new hire in a junior role, it's all too easy to coast or hang back and leave the heavy lifting to someone else. Indeed, that sometimes seems like the default strategy of many office colleagues. But if you mean to survive and thrive in a competitive office environment, and if you mean to do so with the two-strikes-against-you "disadvantage" of being the boss's daughter, you'll need to work harder than everyone else. Establish yourself as the go-to person in your office, the individual who is willing to take on the more onerous tasks that your coworkers shrink from. There's no better way to fit in and make an immediate impression. If your boss needs someone to call on a notoriously difficult client and all the others in your office are coming up with excuses on why they shouldn't be the one, volunteer to make the call. Let your boss see that you're willing to take on the difficult or mundane tasks—and let everyone else see it, too.

Understand, there's a fine line here: you don't want to raise your hand for every assignment in a brown-nosing sort of way. Nobody likes a toady in the workplace. But it's perfectly acceptable and appropriate to take on a little bit more than your share and to set yourself up as a team player. And it's perfectly acceptable and appropriate to let yourself shine a little brighter than the person sitting next to you who cowers whenever your boss approaches with extra work. Just be sure you don't take on more than you can handle, or that you don't steal anyone else's shine; give credit where it's due, but make sure you get the light you deserve.

I recognize that there are unpleasant tasks in every workplace that even senior management types look to avoid—difficult clients, grueling business trips, general grunt work. I'm like most people in that I tend to procrastinate whenever I'm facing a disagreeable assignment, so I've made it a special point to motivate myself in this area. Every morning, I make a list of all the things I expect to accomplish that day, and I place the most difficult, most onerous tasks at the very top of the stack. Over the years, I've found that when I get into the habit of taking on the toughest jobs first, they don't feel so intimidating after a while. When I let those jobs sit on my to-do list, they tend to grow more and more daunting as the day unwinds until I can finally scratch them off and move on.

The lesson: be willing to slog through all the stuff at the bottom, at the first opportunity, if you want to make it to the top.

Don't get caught on the other side of this equation. For every employee who makes a positive impression by unflinchingly taking on the tough tasks, there are many more who make a negative impression by looking to avoid them. I once worked with someone who made himself obsolete by stalling or begging off every time I brought him an undesirable assignment. Instead of diving into the job and assembling and assessing the information I needed, he would let the project file sit on his desk for as long as possible, unopened. He dodged my phone calls whenever I checked in for an update, and when I'd finally corner him he'd pepper me with excuses instead of providing me with the answers I sought. The most frustrating, inexplicable aspect of this pattern of behavior was that this individual wasn't avoiding the work because he was unskilled or incompetent or because the assignments were beyond his capability. Not at all. He simply didn't like addressing some of the more mundane or burdensome aspects of his job—so he didn't, at least not in a timely manner. He got away with it for a while, when the economy was strong and we could afford to overlook his shortcomings in this one regard and focus on his many other strengths, but as soon as we needed to cut costs and trim our payroll, he was the first to go.

My mother had a great trick to get me past a difficult hurdle. When I was little, she'd occasionally host cocktail parties in our apartment in Trump Tower. Something would invariably pull her away when it came time for her guests to arrive, so it usually fell to me to welcome the guests into our home. It was pretty stressful, the first few times this happened, but I got used to it. I learned to keep everyone's name straight and to remember little snippets of our past conversations and layer them onto our current ones. I learned to be a good and gracious host, collecting people's coats and taking their drink orders. Soon I was rushing happily to answer the door in my mother's absence, eager to give our guests a tour of the apartment and start chatting them up, so much so that I'd barely notice when my mother finally made her appearance.

Years later, my mother confessed that she'd always concocted these excuses so as to arrive at her parties "respectably" late. Not because she wanted to make some sort of grand entrance but because she wanted me to be comfortable talking to adults in a sophisticated social setting. She thought it would instill in me a certain poise or confidence, and I suppose it did. Sometimes she'd just remain in her bedroom while I filled in as hostess, working on my social skills without really realizing it.

Even today, my father likes to give me a gentle push, in a sink-or-swim sort of way. Not long after I joined the company, I accompanied him to a press conference in Chicago to give the local press an update on the status of our formidable tower. I was only just beginning to get my feet wet on the project, but I tagged along to get a sense of what things were like in the swirl of media attention that tended to surround my father and the public launch of one of our properties, as well as to get better acquainted with the city itself. It turned out that my father had another agenda. He picked up the microphone to begin the press conference, but before he got too far past his opening remarks he said, "My daughter, Ivanka, will take it from here."

Now, "from here" basically meant after he'd thanked everyone for coming. "From here" meant the responsibility would be on me from there on out. There were hundreds of reporters looking for insight and information, and I was completely unprepared to address them on all aspects of the job. All I knew about the project was what I'd been able to learn through a handful of introductory meetings with the development team during my first month on the job. The best I could manage were a dozen or so "talking points" I'd picked up from our press release or overheard in our hallways back in the office. Talk about a sink-or-swim moment!

I had no choice but to swim—and to fit myself in, in whatever way I could. To project confidence and speak from the heart about our vision for the tower and the impact we hoped it would have on the city.

My father actually winked at me as I stepped to the microphone, and I remember being so pissed that he'd ambushed me—but I couldn't stay mad at him for long. He was just trying to get me to feel comfortable talking in front of a crowd, even when I had no idea what to say. I didn't think he had to be so mischievous about it, but I muddled through. I even ended up answering a few questions with something resembling aplomb, and when it was over I stepped away from the podium and whispered to my father, "What the hell was *that* all about?"

"I just wanted to see how you'd do under pressure, Ivanka," he said, smiling. "Turns out you're good in the clutch."

It was as if we were living inside a Nike ad: *Just do it.* Only here it carried a challenging kicker: *Just do it, even when you're not prepared.*

That's how my parents were with all three of us kids. They'd throw us in at the deep end and take great pride in watching us make it safely to the other side. They knew how important it was for each us to be a little fearless when we were out of our depth. They knew we'd find ourselves in situations where it would feel as if we were in over our heads but we'd have to power past that fear if we hoped to be successful.

They came by the approach naturally. They'd been there, done that when *they* were just starting out. Many people, including my grandfather, thought my father was in way over his head when he decided as a young man to go into the Manhattan real estate market. And as a young Czech immigrant living half a world away from her family, there must have been many moments when my mother wondered if she had strayed too far from her comfort zone when she first came to New York City. Yet both refused to let their doubts or uncertainties get in the way of their dreams.

I've seen this kind of push to perform among some of our most valued employees. Some of them appeared to be overmatched when they began at Trump—but they rose to every opportunity. My parents were always big believers in taking a chance on someone at work, because they knew they themselves wouldn't have gotten where they were if someone hadn't taken a chance on them. I try to do the same. Indeed, at Trump, we believe in identifying and fostering talent from within, and we often find that talent in not-so-obvious places. Someone might start out working for me as an administrative assistant, but if she demonstrates talent and sound judgment I won't hesitate to give her more responsibilities. For instance, if she is creative by nature, I might place her with my marketing team. If she struggles, I'll find a way to ease her back to something more in line with what she'd been doing originally; if she does well, I'll give her even more responsibility. Before long, a career that at first might have been limited by inexperience might morph into something far more rewarding—for the individual *and* for the company.

All across the corporate landscape, there are individuals who might be in the right organization but are stuck in the wrong job. They might be drivers, receptionists, clerks, or even middle managers who lack the platform to showcase their abilities. That's why I'm constantly on the lookout for employees who merit an extra push and an extra layer of responsibility, because it's worth taking risks on someone who comes across as having raw talent. If it works out, you'll receive the boundless loyalty and enthusiasm of a productive, dedicated employee. If it doesn't quite go as planned, you can dial back in such a way that the employee can still be a valued part of your team.

Not too long ago, someone from our security department came to me for advice on how to break into the real estate game now that he was graduating from college. I was impressed by him and the initiative he had taken, so I placed him under the wing of my head of construction. I thought, What's the worst that can happen? This was a bright, hungry, intelligent individual. His questions were thoughtful; his strategy, aggressive. He'd obviously taken the job in security because he knew it would get his foot in the door at our company. Plus I knew he'd work his butt off for me, because I'd given him a shot. It's not as if I was putting him in charge of our construction management division. I just wanted to give him a chance and see if he might be able to meaningfully contribute in this area. So far he has!

How can you stand out in such a way that your boss will be willing to take a chance on you? The first order of business is to take care of business; be sure to do the job you currently have to the best of your ability. If you're working at a fashion magazine as a marketing assistant and it's your not-so-secret ambition to write for the magazine, you'll still have to make yourself indispensable as an assistant before anyone will give you a shot on the editorial side. Too often, I come across talented young people who seem a little too eager to make their marks. If they feel overqualified for the job they're in, they adopt a going-through-the-motions attitude. But if you phone it in on Job

One, you'll never get the call for the job you actually want. In other words, if you set out to show your boss that you're "more" than a secretary, you'll send the message that you believe your current job is somehow beneath you. You might not even realize you're doing it. You might be unprofessional in answering the phone, lax in relaying messages, or careless with your filing.

Here's a textbook example of someone going after her dreams in a purposeful way: A friend of mine worked in Manhattan as an assistant to the editor of a local newspaper. Every day, she'd stay after work and e-mail her boss editorial pitches for the features section. Finally, after a year of dogged determination and a couple of successful freelance assignments to show for her effort, the editor hired her as a writer—and cited her as an example to the rest of the staff of what it took to climb the newsroom ladder. Do your job, he said. And strive for more at the same time.

Don't get too frustrated. No one likes to be stuck doing something she's not passionate about. No one wants to feel her job is beneath her. Realize that your time will come. It might not come on your timetable, but it will come—and until it does you'll be smart to kick butt on whatever it is you're asked to do at the company, even if it seems to have nothing to do with what you want to do next. This doesn't mean that you should bide your time or spin your wheels in a dead-end job with no hope of advancement. If there are no opportunities on the horizon, move on. But if the opportunities are there and all you have to do is get past a few hurdles to grab them, be prepared to spend some time navigating your way over any obstacles.

No one expects you to be trapped in an entry-level position forever, but your boss has every reason to expect you to do a solid job while you're there. Once you establish yourself as a stellar young professional and you've managed to build good relationships with your peers and supervisors, it's appropriate to start dropping hints that you'd be interested in doing more. Still at the hypothetical fashion magazine cited above, you might mention that you used to write for your college newspaper. Or that you recently took a class in fashion design or marketing at a local university. Put it out there that you have a background in editorial and a real interest in fashion, and see what happens. Be prepared to give it some time. If nothing shakes out after a reasonable period, it's okay to be a little more straightforward in your approach. Drop bigger hints. Or come right out and ask your boss if she could help arrange an interview for you with the managing editor or someone in editorial.

Chances are, a strong manager will recognize that you can be an even greater asset to the magazine and that your continued success will contribute to her success as well. If she snubs you, you'll get a clear message that this is not the right environment for you if you hope to move up and out of your current position.

BE YOUR SUNDAY BEST

I'm always looking for an edge, and I find a great big one at the start of every workweek. For as long as I can remember, I've been in the habit of coming into the office on Sundays, when things are relatively quiet and I can get more done in a few hours than I can in a full day crammed with meetings and conference calls and the usual interoffice logjam.

I came to this tactic on my own, but it was ratified for me early on by no less a role model than Rupert Murdoch, the Australian-born media mogul and chairman of News Corp. I'm fortunate to count Rupert among my friends, one of the many I've developed over the years independent of my family contacts. We met for brunch one Sunday and were joined by Robert Thomson, then the publisher of *The Wall Street Journal*, along with Dow Jones CEO Les Hinton and Rupert's wife, Wendi. This was just after Rupert had purchased the paper, when pundits were predicting the demise of the venerable broadsheet at the hands of the media baron. Of course, this turned out not to be the case, and the *Journal* has flourished editorially under Rupert's control, but at the time he was getting beaten up in the press (his competition!) for taking over such a respected and beloved publication.

As we parted that afternoon, Rupert asked what I had planned for the rest of the day. It was a beautiful winter day, so I mentioned that I was thinking about taking a walk through Central Park or maybe meeting up with friends later on. "What about you?" I asked.

"Robert, Les, and I are going to head down to the *Journal*," Rupert said. "We'll see what we find."

What they most likely found on that beautiful Sunday afternoon was a nearly deserted newsroom—but that wouldn't be the case for long. *Journal* staffers, other than the ones charged with getting out the Monday edition, weren't used to working on Sundays, but once Rupert started showing up on Sundays the culture of the newsroom began to change. Soon even some of his most senior employees were making a point of dropping by the office on weekends. Nobody had to tell them do to so; they just knew that if their boss was going to be there, they'd better be there, too.

Like Rupert, I try to stop by my office every Sunday when I'm in town. I might stay for only an hour or two, but I find it to be such a relaxing, focused time. I'll race through the paperwork and correspondence that tends to pile up on my desk and get organized for the week ahead. If there's nothing else going on, I'll even make a few calls and catch up on my e-mails—especially if I have reason to think the people I'm reaching out to might be at their desks, too. (They often are!) Then, after I'm done, the rest of my Sunday is more relaxing and stress-free than if I hadn't made the effort.

I understand that going in to the office can be a drag—but that's a mind-set. A *negative* mind-set. If you flip it around, you can make it a positive. Turn your office into a haven of opportunity, and it can become a kind of magnet, a place where you're drawn to feel good about yourself and everything you might accomplish. I admit that there have been many lazy Sunday mornings when I've woken up and wanted to do nothing else but lie around my apartment for the rest of the day.

But if I think going in to the office will put me in a better position on Monday morning and prepare me for the week ahead, then I find a way to get there.

Now, I don't carry the kind of influence that Rupert Murdoch wields around the *Journal* newsroom, and I certainly don't require the people who work for me to follow my lead on this, but you'd be surprised at how quickly your employees will fall in line behind you when you set this kind of example. I like to think they're doing so for their own self-starting, self-motivating reasons and because good habits tend to rub off on others, although I realize there's a certain element of point scoring involved. There's nothing wrong with that. It gets the job done, it keeps my entire team one step ahead, and it helps me to evaluate intangibles such as commitment and dedication and all those good things. When I see one of my employees at her desk on a Sunday morning, I'll stop to chat for a while. But if I start to see her consistently, she'll know I've taken note. I might bring her a cup of coffee or grab us lunch, and that way she'll get the subtle message that her extra efforts are noticed and appreciated.

I take great pride in the fact that my brothers and I are typically the first ones in to the office every morning and the last ones to leave every night. If an employee wants to catch my eye, matching that effort is a great way to do so. I will certainly notice if someone consistently beats me into the office each morning and is there to wish me good night when I head home at seven-thirty or so. If he struggles in other areas, you can be sure I'll take his extra effort into account when I evaluate his performance.

Showing up is half the battle. Showing up early, staying late, or working weekends can make up a big chunk of the other half. It can cover a lot of ground for you when you put in the time that others aren't willing to invest. You might not be as articulate or as charming as your coworkers. You might not have their Ivy League pedigrees or their advanced degrees. But there's no reason you can't get to work earlier than they do every morning and leave later every evening.

There's no reason you can't be behind your desk on Sundays while they're watching college football or drinking mimosas with their friends. That's one of the great things about most work environments: they're not exactly the most level playing fields, and the easiest way to tilt things to your advantage is to put in the time. You might not be able to match your colleagues in every category, but you can surpass them when it comes to hard work.

To be sure, all this hard work comes with a price. Unless you're superhuman, your social life will likely suffer—but it's important to remember that your age-appropriate social life will be just fine. As a young professional, you shouldn't be out partying all night, the way you might have in college. Once in a while, okay. But you'll need to start thinking about getting a good night's sleep and coming in to the office each day feeling fresh instead of trashed. For me, this wasn't such a challenge, because my extracurricular pursuits have always been pretty mellow. I'd rather have a casual dinner with friends or hang out at home and watch a movie than go out clubbing or barhopping. It's just not my thing. If it's yours, that's fine, but keep things in perspective.

That said, my friends still drag me out dancing every once in a while, and I'm (almost) always glad when they do. We have a blast. But it would wear me down if I went out like that every Thursday night. There's just no way you can be at your desk first thing on Friday morning, physically yes but mentally no, if you've been out all night drinking and partying.

Know your limits. Know your responsibilities. And know that if you can't count on yourself to make the correct choices when it comes to finding the right balance between work and play, your boss won't be able to count on you, either.

That edge we all seek, to get and keep ahead? It can't find you out on the town, drinking yourself into oblivion, but it will be there waiting for you at your desk bright and early each day—Sundays, too.

BULLETINS FROM MY BLACKBERRY

DANY LEVY—Founder, chairman, and editorial director, DailyCandy.com

ON MANAGING YOUR TEAM

I firmly believe that to be an effective leader you need to remember what it was like to have been an employee. To have been that scrappy little newbie on the bottom rung who answers phones, wrangles with the broken copy machine, makes coffee, and, most important, watches what goes on around the office. That's where you learn the stuff they don't (and can't) teach in school—such as what makes an office and its colorful cast of characters tick. That was me, starting out, and along the way I had every kind of boss you can imagine. Crazy, wonderful, and everything in between. Collectively, those experiences helped me discover the kind of boss I wanted to be. Somewhere between crazy and great, I guess, but hopefully leaning toward great.

I also learned what I didn't like about office culture. I learned that I often found meetings counterproductive and something of a time suck, so now I keep them to a minimum. And I love them short. I have a term I like to use: "hard stop." I'll open a meeting and say I have a "hard stop" at ten. That way everyone knows to stay on point, because at ten o'clock we're done.

I've also developed a sensitive radar for the pettiness, backstabbing, and cattiness you sometimes find in the workplace. My big thing is that everyone on my team should be pulling for one another. We are in it together. We've got each other's backs. I insist on this. Everything flows from the top. I have no tolerance for managers or leaders who take credit for other people's work. The flip side bothers me, too, when people are quick to blame someone on their staff when something goes wrong. I'm also really not interested in the whole "Wow, look at me!" power aspect of being that jazzes some people. It's self-involved and egotistical and does nothing to advance the task at hand.

Perhaps the hardest part of being a boss is learning how to offer constructive criticism. I like to use what I call it the "criticism sandwich": I take whatever needs improvement and wrap it between two pieces of praise. Something good, something not so good, something good. That feels like the right balance.

Basically, it's important to be kind. It goes a long way in this world. Treat people the way you'd like to be treated. Do unto others, right? It sounds simple, but people so often lose sight of the basics. Lose that, and you're toast.

EIGHT

NAVIGATING THE WORKPLACE

The learned man knows that he is ignorant.

—VICTOR HUGO

I consider myself a student of human behavior, and a career in business offers the perfect petri dish for me to observe all kinds of people, in all kinds of professional situations, going through all kinds of motions to get and stay ahead. I take note when one strategy works and another one fails and constantly stay on the lookout for new approaches that might yield even the slightest edge.

After all, we don't get ahead by moving forward recklessly. We get there by degrees, one painstaking step at a time.

These days, that often means learning how to manage our technology in such a way that it doesn't end up managing us. With our handheld devices and desktop feeds and twenty-four-hour information overload, there's never been a time when we've been more connected to one another—yet I can't stop thinking that there's more and more of a disconnect in the traditional workplace environment. It cuts along generational lines, for the most part, and among the younger segment of our workforce, technology has changed the ways we communicate with one another, not always to the good. We've

149

become so accustomed to being constantly plugged in to each other and to the world around that the resulting onslaught of news and information and Tweets can get in the way of basic human interaction. It's no longer unusual to see someone walking down the hallway or headed for the elevator talking wirelessly and breathlessly into a Bluetooth-type device, but each time I do, I still catch myself thinking there's a crazy person coming my way, mumbling some inanity or other. I've used those devices myself from time to time, but if you're not in on the conversation it's all too easy to think you've stumbled upon some psychotic episode.

It used to be said that the most successful, most motivated, most ambitious entrepreneurs were wired to work. Now we're just wired—and I sometimes wonder if we haven't gotten our wires crossed along the way. Consider what it means when we try to do too much, all at once. Multitasking has become the rallying cry of my generation, and we wear it like a badge of honor. The more balls we can keep in the air at one time, the better. The more we can manage, the more we can become. At least that's the theory.

For years, I prided myself on my ability to walk and chew gum at the same time—in a business sense, of course. I could be on a conference call with bankers in Asia, e-mailing the general manager of one of our hotels, and scanning the morning newspapers, all at the same time. Not bad, huh? A lot of my friends were at their desks all across the city, doing their version of the same thing. Some of them would even keep a game of Brickbreaker or Solitaire going on one of their computer screens, to fill the few fleeting moments they managed to steal between more consequential tasks.

But then I started to realize that the more I tried to do, the less I actually accomplished. It took me awhile to come to this view, but now I see that by spreading myself so thin I was wasting an important opportunity by not giving the task at hand my full attention. I'd be present on a conference call, but too distracted by everything else

I was doing to participate fully. I'd hit the "send" button on an e-mail, but I probably didn't communicate my point as precisely as I'd intended. And I'd thumbed through the paper and skimmed a few articles, but I couldn't have shared anything I'd just read with any sort of authority.

Gradually, I came to the conclusion that multitasking is a drag on productivity. Anyway, it's a drag on mine. Of course, our fast-paced, instant-information culture has set things up so we have no choice but to do more than one thing at a time if we hope to keep pace, but I try to curb my multitasking impulses. Why? They sap me of my ability to focus. They redirect me from what I should be doing. They're the polar opposite of what we've taken to calling "senior moments," when an older person might momentarily lose his or her place in a conversation and attribute it to age or senility. They're "junior moments," when younger executives momentarily lose *their* places because they have one conversation going on in their ear, another at their fingertips, and still another across the conference table. We're a little too quick to attribute these gaps to technology; in truth, they're just a sign of our rampant inability to pay close and careful attention to any one thing for any extended period—or even for the briefest period, in some cases.

Multitasking is not a dirty word. In fact, I'm always trying to juggle many different projects and initiatives. On any given day, there's a long list of urgent matters competing for my time and attention. This is a good thing—and it keeps me sharp and agile. But when I'm unable to concentrate on the task at hand because I'm trying to answer an e-mail and at the same time giving directions to my assistant or paying attention to the stock market ticker on the television screen in my office . . . then I start to lose my focus.

My father has no patience for all the electronic gadgets that hypnotize the younger generation in the workforce. He considers them distractions. He hates how my brothers and I have so many drags on our attention—and he's right. Plus, he practices what he preaches. He doesn't even have a computer on his desk. He doesn't carry a Black-Berry. He only reluctantly carries a cell phone. He focuses completely on the task in front of him—and he expects his children and the rest of his team to do the same. He values doing business one-on-one, whether in person or over the phone. I agree with him, but only to a degree. There's a time and place for every technological advance-ment—as long as we don't use them everywhere and all at once. Used appropriately, technology can be a godsend. When I travel, for exam-ple, I can read e-mails off my handheld device and be available to offer a quick answer to a pressing problem.

Still, it drives my father nuts if he's talking to me about a project and catches my eyes gravitating toward the BlackBerry in my hand. It's one of the only reasons he'll yell at me at work. "Ivanka!" he'll roar. "Put that freaking thing down!"

TECH TIPS TO KEEP LIFE SANE

Over time, my father got through to me on this, and I now try to keep my "junior moments" to a minimum. If I'm in an important meeting, I'll leave my BlackBerry in my bag—and definitely *not* on the confer-ence table in front of me!—because I know that even if I'm sitting across from a group of bankers who hold the fate of a new project in their hands, I might not be able to resist the siren call of that blinking red light, telling me a new e-mail is waiting. (Go ahead, tell me you've never sneaked a peek under a conference table in an important meet-ing at some trivial e-mail or text message.) I've come to appreciate that there's no piece of incoming information that could possibly be more important than the exchange of information and ideas unfold-ing right in front of me—or at least no piece that can't wait until the meeting is over to give it my full attention.

Once I placed a shoebox marked "CrackBerries" on a side table in our conference room before one of our regular Monday-morning

"New Deal" meetings. These meetings are attended by our entire development team, but I'd noticed that they were becoming less and less productive as more and more of them were constantly tapping away on their handheld devices. So I half jokingly hit on this solution—and it worked! I collected everyone's BlackBerrys as the meeting was getting under way, and we shot through our agenda a full half hour ahead of schedule. And it was more than just a time-saver. People were more focused and less likely to repeat what others had already said, because they had no choice but to pay attention.

Yes, it's important to stay connected with colleagues and clients—it's essential!—but it's even more important to keep connected to your work. Think about it: When was the last time you spent one uninterrupted hour working on a project? When you unplugged the phone, powered down your gadgets, and shut your office door so you could *really* study a report or review a contract or consider a proposal? Be honest. Chances are it hasn't happened in a long time. (And if you're under thirty, there's a good chance it's *never* happened!) Even when you think you're putting your nose to the grindstone on a project, you're probably checking your e-mail every now and then or updating your Facebook page, or responding to an instant message. (This is one of the reasons why I make my way into the office every Sunday—to focus on big-picture initiatives away from all the small interruptions!)

Lately, I've come up with a few strategies to keep all these distractions at bay:

Check your BlackBerry or iPhone only on the quarter hour. Even if that blinking red lights keeps calling to you, don't give in. There are very few e-mails that can't wait fifteen minutes for you to respond. Keep your eye on the prize, and don't get bogged down with minutiae. Getting a handle on the frequency of your e-mail checks will keep you from dropping the ball on a matter of consequence.

Always respond to phone calls within twenty-four hours. I like to respond in the order in which the calls were received. It doesn't matter if it's a contractor or a U.S. senator.

Swim in one information stream at a time. If you're sitting on your couch at home, working on your laptop, turn off the television. If you're on a conference call, don't put your phone on mute so that you can IM your friend without the other parties hearing you *tap, tap, tap* on your keyboard. (Okay, maybe I've done this a few times, so I know the drill—but it's a bad idea.) Don't fall into the destructive habit of having several things going on at once, because then all you have is a bunch of background noise, and your attention will never be front and center, where it belongs.

Keep your responses to a minimum. We've all been caught in an endless e-mail or text exchange, where one party is constantly posing open-ended questions or sending a message that calls for some sort of reply. Or maybe there's a long string of e-mails being passed among a large group, with no resolution in sight. If I'm engaged in an e-mail back-and-forth that fails to reach a conclusion in a timely manner, I'll request a quick meeting or schedule a phone call to put the issue to bed—especially if there's a ton of people on the e-mail chain.

Even better: don't respond. Not every message requires your immediate attention. Some don't rate a response at all. Figure it out, and respond accordingly. Or not at all.

Don't sleep with your BlackBerry next to your bed. I've been guilty of this for a while, but I'm trying to break the habit. It helps that people know they can reach me until around 11 P.M. and then again as early as 6 A.M., so now I turn the device off overnight.

Keep your BlackBerry or iPhone in your bag or your pocket when you're out to eat. This is just plain good manners. I've been to meals where all six people place their BlackBerrys on the table as they're being seated. The waiter can't even find room for the bread basket! But there's more than common courtesy or table real estate to consider here; you might also find that you're more plugged in to the conversation if you're unplugged everywhere else.

Vary your response time. This is one of the best strategies I've learned to counter the heat and haste of our information age. If you consistently return e-mails the moment you receive them, people might read something into it when you don't respond immediately. It might be a sign of trouble or concern or an indication that you weren't happy with the latest proposal. Control their expectations. Mix things up. This can be especially important if you're working on a deal and need some time to think things through. Be accessible, but don't set things up so you're bound to any timetable but your own.

The debate over how and when to make the best use of available technology highlights a broader generational divide in the workplace. My older friends and associates seem to hate our shorter attention spans—"the ADD of youth," they call it—and maintain that texting or IM-ing during meetings is disruptive and disrespectful. My younger friends, however, are conditioned to carry on a conversation with a colleague while they tap away at their BlackBerry keyboards, never making eye contact. Somewhere in the middle is the right place to be.

YOU'VE GOT MAIL!

E-mail etiquette presents its own set of problems. There's a popular misconception that it's okay to be a little less accountable and professional in a dashed-off e-mail message than we might be in a more thoughtful correspondence. I don't accept that line of thought, but I do get these kinds of e-mails all the time. At work, young people tend to use e-mail the way they used to pass notes to each other back in grade school. They whisper their little secrets or snide comments, thinking no one will hear. But our work e-mail isn't anonymous or protected, and it shouldn't be. And it's certainly *not* private. Ultimately, cyberspace is just like any other public space, so it's foolish to act otherwise.

I learned this the hard way, I'm afraid. I used to exchange e-mails with an influential businessman. We were good friends, and we fell into the habit of sending each other funny little articles and jokes, some of them a little bit off color. It was a type of networking, I guess, but it was more social than professional. After a while, I let myself become a little too informal in our exchanges, and that's when I got into trouble. I'd read an item in the newspaper reporting that my friend had just closed on a particularly good deal in an emerging market. So I shot off a foolish e-mail: "Wow. Great deal. Who got a kickback?"

I didn't think much of it, but I should have. That's the problem with a lot of e-mails sent to and from our places of business—we don't think about them. We don't think about the pictures we post online, either, but that seems like a more obvious point. By now most enterprising young people have learned that they need to filter the portraits they paint of themselves on Facebook, Twitter, and MySpace—because those, too, are fair game. Personally, I *always* look people up online when I'm thinking about hiring them or working with them. It's only a matter of time before some political candidate or high-level appointee is bounced from contention because he or she has been "tagged" in an inappropriate photo.

But loose-lipped, ill-considered e-mails are still a big trouble spot—and here my foolish transmission left me red-cheeked. A few minutes after pressing send, I received a very formal e-mail from my usually casual friend, asking for a written retraction and telling me in no uncertain terms that my comment was inappropriate. After all, he was the CEO of a large, publicly held company, and that stupid message could have caused him serious trouble. I was mortified—and I should have been. My behavior was unprofessional and just plain stupid. I spent the rest of the day wondering how I could have been so careless.

Rule of thumb: if you're not comfortable saying something in a conference room, in front of your boss, or even in a roomful of strangers, don't write it in an e-mail; you might as well hire a small plane and unfurl your message from a banner outside your office windows. Even if you think the comment is fairly benign, you never know how it might appear out of context, and once you press "Send" you're no longer in control of that context. You might make a similarly flippant remark in casual conversation, but then at least you're somewhat certain of the situation. Then you can determine how and when your comment is uttered and who might be in earshot. With an e-mail, however, you can never be certain how widely it might be circulated or how you'll come across—so you're better off refraining.

My friend Andrew Cuomo, New York's great attorney general, tells me that e-mail is the key to prosecuting just about everyone these days. People are so incredibly slapdash with their electronic messages, as if they were some modern version of smoke signals that can disappear without a trace. Indeed, it's just the opposite: e-mail correspondence can be retrieved in perpetuity, so there's no hiding from what you've written in haste or hoping it goes away. Text messages have a slightly shorter shelf life, but they can still be incriminating. I'm sure some techie out there can hack his or her way into your cell transmissions going back years and years.

It's not just the messages you send that should have you concerned; it's the one's you receive. Let's face it—you don't want to be associated with questionable language or behavior or judgment, even if you're not guilty of anything more than corresponding with individuals who might see the world a little differently. From time to time, I'll open an e-mail that places me in a vulnerable situation, like the one I had unfortunately placed my previously mentioned friend in, and when that happens, I shoot off a disapproving note in response. "Don't ever copy me on an e-mail like that again," I'll write—or words to that effect. If you don't know me, I might come across as a goodie two-shoes, but that doesn't bother me so much as the thought that someone might open a suggestive e-mail with my name on the cc: list and judge me guilty by association.

Bottom line: we are just as responsible for the e-mails we receive as the ones we send, something to think about when using your work address to communicate with friends. If you and your friends have it set up so this kind of back-and-forth is a central part of your relationship, you should at least be smart about it: use a personal e-mail account so nothing you send or receive can be misconstrued at work.

Another of my concerns regarding our various forms of instant electronic communication is the way it has accelerated the decline of the English language. I cringe whenever I receive an e-mail with improper grammar or teenage shorthand. I'm sorry, but LOL or TTYL—or, the dreaded WTF?—have no place in a professional environment. And emoticons! OMG, what's wrong with all these people, inserting little smiley faces to indicate their happiness or frowny faces to express their displeasure? It's so juvenile, so unprofessional, so inappropriate.

PIT BULLS AND CHIHUAHUAS

Character is key in the workplace, and I'm usually pretty good at identifying the various personality types I encounter in a professional setting. That's why I always tell people to pay careful attention to how they present themselves to their bosses and colleagues, because you never know how or when a pattern of behavior might make it difficult to get out of your own way.

For example, I have two people working for me at the Trump Organization who tend be overanxious. In micro terms, this is not such a bad thing. When an individual employee is overanxious, he or she tends to make an extra effort to get it right, in a meticulous sort of way. Each of these two individuals is a valuable member of my team, and each makes an important contribution, but I sometimes think they're a little too eager for their own good—and ultimately for mine as their manager. They're constantly underfoot, asking questions and looking for feedback and validation of their work. They get the job done and in many cases exceed my expectations, but I tend to think of them as high maintenance. I walk around feeling as if they're tugging at my sleeve, desperate for my attention—whereas in reality they're probably more suited to the tasks they've been assigned than I would be.

Their eagerness extends to taking on new projects, of course—and here again, there's nothing wrong with such fervor and dedication. These two employees take on every task I throw at them. They'll even compete with each other for assignments, in a relatively healthy way. Not too long ago, they both came bouncing into my office after hearing that we had just finalized a deal. Before I could even share any of the details of the project, they were fighting over who would get to work on it. One of them pointed out that she had a strong background in horizontal development, while the other countered that he had just come off a similar project in Turkey and might make a better fit.

I've come to look on these two employees as "pit bulls," because they're so relentless and aggressive in their approach. In that same micro way, pit bulls can be a pleasure to work with. They might not always come from the best schools or have the smoothest social skills, but they get the job done—usually on time and under budget. It's in a macro way that this type of personality can get to be a little too much. Too many pit bulls can make things a little tense and oppressive around the office. There needs to be a balance. When I put together a team on a project, I'll always lean toward a hard-working, aggressive pit bull—but only if I don't already have too many alpha dogs on board.

On the other side of the equation, I have a set of employees who are closer in temperament to chihuahuas. Instead of aggressive and confident, they come across as nervous and meek. Like a lot of people who love big dogs, I tend to find chihuahuas a little annoying, and yet I recognize that if I didn't have at least a few of these types in the mix, our office environment would be too stressful. And so I seek that balance. Those people are hard workers, but they don't strive to be leaders—just great soldiers. That's okay, too. Not everyone can be a deal maker. You need some of your cast to take on supporting roles.

I once had someone working for me who was definitely more chihuahua than pit bull. He was bright and talented, but he was also insecure and somewhat timid in his approach. Instead of taking on each new assignment assertively, he would constantly come right back to me looking for direction—direction I didn't always have the time or patience to offer. Unlike a pit bull, who might be aggressive and assertive in his approach, this individual was extremely timid. Every time we interacted, it felt as if he were asking me a question that didn't really need to be asked. "Ivanka," he'd say, "would you mind reviewing the points in this e-mail before I send it out?" Or "Ivanka, do you think I'm going about this negotiation the right way?" No one question was troubling, but taken together they were a drain. It got to where when I saw this chihuahua coming down the hallway, my instinct was to turn the corner and hide. Instead of my appreciating his intelligence and talents, which were both considerable, his neediness became his defining characteristic. At first I thought he wanted me to task-manage his time. Then I thought I wasn't giving him enough work and this was his passive-aggressive way of telling me he could handle more. In any case, it all added up to too much thought on my part. I wanted to be able to hand off an assignment and know it would get done, so I'm afraid this particular chihuahua didn't last too long in our organization.

When your boss looks at you, does she see a pit bull or a chihuahua? Is your attitude confident and unrelenting? Or is it trembling and uncertain? Do you carefully choose when and how to ask for advice? Or do you simply ask away, even about trivial matters you could probably figure out for yourself? Know your strengths and your weaknesses, and recognize that what might appear as a weakness to one person could be a strength to another. Know, too, that if you notice too many of your "types" in your particular office, you might want to switch things up, because it's tough to stand out when you all look the same. If everyone else in the office has a soft touch, go at your work a little harder.

Personally, I am okay with it when a chihuahua flies under my radar in a stealthy sort of way—as long as I know she's on it, working hard behind the scenes. What doesn't work is a fainthearted employee who hides behind her insecurities and inabilities in such a way that she hopes no one notices them. We've all worked alongside people like that—people who believe that by appearing busy and frantic, they'll give the impression that they're hard at work on the task at hand. As a manager, however, I take the opposite view. When I see a frantic, frazzled employee, I don't think, Here is a person who is absolutely busting her butt. Instead, I think, Gee, maybe this person should calm down. If she weren't so nervous, she might be more productive.

Russell Simmons, the hip-hop mogul, likes to remind his younger employees that stress does not equal hard work. He shared that thought with me one day, and I told him I was going to steal it and put it in my book. He loves the energy young people bring to his organization, he told me, but he has to constantly remind them to channel it more effectively. "I appreciate that these kids want to get it right," he said. "But the mistake they make is thinking that the time they spend worrying about something is the same as actually working on it."

I see that all the time—among both pit bulls and chihuahuas. At the end of the day, my most valued employees are not the ones who pull out their hair and go a little crazy when there's a pile of work on their desk but the ones who actually become more focused and more efficient when things get busy. Some of them do this in a quiet way, and some of them do it in an attention-getting way. It doesn't matter to me. All I care, really, is that they get the job done—and that they do so in such a way that there's balance and harmony. I'm like most managers in this regard, I guess. I don't like it when things are too loud. I don't like it when things are too quiet. I like it when they're just right.

NEGOTIATE EVERYTHING

Yes, everything.

In my life, this means everything from legal bills to real estate deals in Panama. I've been negotiating for as long as I can remember. When I was a student at Choate, I negotiated off-campus privileges to allow me to pursue my modeling career in New York—no easy feat in the traditional boarding school lockdown environment. The school officials were lined up against me on this, but I made a compelling argument. They'd granted similar leave to a student who was training to be an Olympic skier, so I used precedent to my advantage and got what I wanted, which included keeping a car on campus and getting permission to drive down to New York for go-sees. One of the great lessons here was that my parents left it to me to work out the terms. If it was something I wanted, they knew I'd find a way to make it happen.

That's what you're doing when you're banging out an agreement—you're finding a way to make something happen: a transaction, a contract, an arrangement of some kind or other. The best negotiations result in a deal that benefits both parties, so very often that's what I try to accomplish. Of course, there are times when you simply want to come out ahead in a deal, but as a guiding principle you'll want to play it straight, because you never know when you'll next be seated across the table from the very same person, working on a follow-up transaction. The only time I stray from this philosophy is when I'm angling for some kind of break on a personal level or when the residual relationship is irrelevant. I'll call to renegotiate my cable bill, for example, if I hear that a friend in my building is paying far less for her service. Here I'm not looking to build or nurture a relationship, the way I would be in a professional negotiation. Instead, I'm looking to get the best price for the same service. I'm offering the cable company the continued privilege of doing business with me, a long-term customer. What I'm seeking is simply the courtesy of being given the same terms it has extended to others—and preferably better.

A lot of people think it's tacky to negotiate with a vendor. They even have a name for it: haggling. But I don't see anything wrong with the practice. There's no negative taint to it; as far as I'm concerned, it's just business. For the longest time, there were certain settings where negotiating on a sales price was considered unacceptable—in department stores, for example. Yet in marketplaces all around the world, haggling over price is the order of the day. It's the law of supply and demand. Here in the United States, it's perfectly acceptable, even expected, for us to negotiate in some circumstances—say, when shopping for a new car. And now, as our economy tightens, we're seeing this type of negotiation more and more, as consumers are less and less inclined to part with their hard-earned dollars, and sellers are becoming increasingly eager to pry those dollars from customers' fingers.

My father is well known for his negotiating skills, so I've been fortunate enough to learn from the very best. A great many so-called experts have written volumes on the subject, but here are a couple of pointers I've picked up along the way.

Know what you want. It's the number one rule going into any negotiation, yet most people don't give it a thought. They'll start in on a series of discussions and figure their objectives will become clear to them in time. If you take this approach you'll allow the other party to define your goals, instead of the other way around.

Be aware of your physical presence. Size matters. Height, stature, how you carry yourself—they all come into play in a negotiation. In some cases the balance of power is already tilted in one direction before discussions even began. I once read about an executive who had his desk built six inches too high (with a desk chair perched at a corresponding height), placed opposite a visitor's chair that was six inches too low. I don't advocate this approach, but I appreciate the message behind it: a show of strength can very often be misinterpreted as . . . well, strength. The effect in this scenario was to put the executive in a clear position of power and authority over his visitor—to make his opposition feel "dominated" from the outset. Talk about home-field advantage!

Make sure you're negotiating with the right person. A classic rookie mistake is you make all kinds of progress and give all kinds of concessions, and suddenly you look up and realize the person you're talking to doesn't have the authority to finalize your deal. The actual "boss" will then come to the table and continue the negotiation, often without acknowledging the concessions you have already made.

Try to read the people across the table from you. Put yourself in their shoes. Think about what makes sense for them in this deal. Think about the points they might be unwilling to concede—and why.

Understand their personality. Collect as much information as you can about the people you'll be dealing with. Learn what they're *really* looking to get out of the deal, not just what they're telling you. Discover their true goal, and you'll be well on your way to yours. The best way to do this is to listen more than you speak. You might discover a concession you can make that will cost you only a little and count for a lot on the other side. Know that some people respond better to a carrot; others, to a stick. Know which type of person you're dealing with, and alter your style to suit. Be the carrot or be the stick, but get it done.

Be honest with yourself. Know that your personality will sometimes clash with the other party and that it's okay to separate yourself from the negotiation if you think your involvement is counterproductive. Remember, it's not about you, it's about the deal. Bring in another member of your team if you find yourself at an impasse. Don, Eric, and I are always sizing up our "competition" on the other side of the table to determine which one of us might be best suited to a particular negotiation.

Understand that people ask for more than they expect to get. Feel free to do the same. My brother Don is always reminding me that you don't get what you don't ask for.

Share the logic for your requests. If your fellow negotiator understands your reasoning, and your logic is sound, it makes it more difficult to oppose the request.

Trust, but verify. I'm always prepared to give someone the benefit of the doubt, but I'm careful to back it up during the due diligence process. A certain amount of skepticism is healthy in assessing the merits of any deal.

Resist the temptation to cut the pie in half. Make trades, but don't think that splitting the difference down the middle is any kind of winning solution to a stalemate. Demonstrate a willingness to do so, and it will lead to bad behavior on the other side. The other party will end up asking for too much in order to anchor you at a higher number, making it difficult for you to bridge the gap in a workable way.

Don't negotiate by e-mail. It might seem like a convenient time-saver, but it's a cop-out. In my experience, it actually benefits the weaker party, because that person will be able to avoid a direct confrontation and have more time to craft a strong response to their weak position.

Give to get. The best deal is the one that works out favorably for both parties—except in a pure buy-sell transaction with no like-lihood of future deals. I try to keep this in mind when I'm work-ing on a new partnership agreement or some type of joint venture. A lot of times, you'll continue to work with the other party long after your deal is finalized, so it's in everyone's best interest to make sure each side believes it got a good deal. I never mind it when the other guy feels as if he "won" a particular ne-gotiation, because if I'm happy with the outcome and it satisfies my company's goals, I'll know it means that I won as well.

Perception is more important than reality. If someone per-ceives something to be true, it is more important than if it is in fact true. Let the other guy think what he wants. This doesn't mean you should be duplicitous or deceitful, but don't go out of your way to correct a false assumption if it plays to your advan-tage.

Put all your big issues on the table. Right away, if you can. The longer you wait to show your hand, the fewer cards you'll have to play.

Make sure your concessions are acknowledged. Even if they're relatively small. It'll help your case later on if the other guys feel as if they've won a point or two.

Use your leverage. I'm not afraid to use my celebrity to my advantage in negotiations. Or my connections. Very often, when I'm trying to seal a favorable deal, I'll invite a potential partner to one of our country clubs for a friendly round of golf. Sometimes the smallest "sweetener" can produce the biggest results; it softens the other guy up and puts him in a position to want to respond favorably to me and my terms.

Be prepared. The Boy Scouts know what they're doing. Do your homework, and come to the table armed with research, backstory, and whatever other information you can find. The more you know, the stronger your position. It's tough to argue with someone who can back up her assertions with a rational, knowledgeable argument.

Know when to walk away. Some of the best deals I ever negotiated are the ones that never came to fruition. Lately, I've been very fortunate to have walked away from several top-of-the-market deals that just didn't make sense for us at the time. That they would make even less sense for us now is a victory of a kind. One thing I always try to maintain is what I call my "walk-away power." Let it be known that you're perfectly willing to let a deal go if you can't make it work. If the other guy thinks you're forced by circumstances to do a deal, he'll have an advantage.

Don't allow negotiations to drag on too long. Many a deal dies under its own weight. It still might be a good deal all around, but human nature gets in the way. People lose their passion for a transaction that never quite reaches its conclusion, especially entrepreneurial types, if they start to think you want to beat them up on every nonsubstantive issue.

Negotiating strategies come into play within your work environment as well, as you collaborate with your colleagues and supervisors.

One of the most nerve-racking rites of passage for any young worker is negotiating your own raise—or attempting to. In my case, my nerves are especially shot when it's time to ask for a bump in pay because I have to go up against my father, who prides himself on being a tough negotiator. I always assumed this meant he'd be especially tough on me—and he surely has been.

The first time around, I actually had to demonstrate my value to the company in real terms. It was about a year after I'd started working for him, and I felt it was time for a raise, so I looked at every deal I'd worked on, every project I'd helped develop, every initiative I'd put into play. I attempted to quantify each effort in an attempt to get my father to see that he'd been employing me at a bargain rate for the previous year. He really put me through my paces—and he continues to do so. Sometimes I get what I want; other times I don't. But my father has almost always been right in his assessment. He might not have always given me the raise I wanted, but he usually gave me the raise I deserved.

This opening salary dance with my father taught me an important lesson about evaluating your worth in a company: don't be afraid to let your bosses know that you're doing good things. Too often, you find young employees unwilling to take credit for their contributions. They're raised to believe it's not polite to call attention to themselves, but that type of modesty never really cut it in our household—and it certainly doesn't cut it in the Trump Organization. It's one thing to be part of a team, but in a salary review you'll need to grab what's yours. I grew up in an environment where I was encouraged to own my accomplishments, and that carried over into the family business as well. And I learned during my short time at Forest City and a handful of internships never to assume that my immediate bosses knew the full extent of my contributions at work, because there are always people who will try to take credit for something you've done. If your direct superior is the one taking the credit, don't be afraid to go over his head and claim your due. Develop a strategic approach, but tread lightly.

You'll need to have your contribution acknowledged and appreciated by the people in a position to promote you, without alienating your direct superior. If you are unwilling or unable to step out of the shadow of a boss who stifles your growth and fails to give you credit for the fruit of your efforts, you'll probably have to leave the company and start over someplace else. It's essential to get out from under a mid-level boss who looks to marginalize your work.

Early jobs also taught me the importance of picking your moments. I won't go to my father for a raise if I see he's in a sour mood, just as I'm disinclined to respond favorably when one of my own employees comes to me to ask for a raise at the end of a really bad day. With my father, I'll check in with his secretary to see how things are going. I'll consult his calendar to make sure we won't be pressed for time if I drop in on him unannounced. I'll also try to have the conversation when things are going well for our company in general, or after we've closed a big deal that I'd worked on. If you ask for a raise during a recession or a prolonged downturn, your request could backfire, so it makes sense to be sensitive to market conditions.

One final point: accept the fact that time served doesn't automatically qualify you for a raise. I run into this type of thinking all the time, and it sets me off. If you're making the same contributions to the company in year five that you made in year one, you don't deserve a raise. You should be happy that you still have a job.

MARK BURNETT—Television producer

ON KEEPING YOUR WORD

I first met Donald Trump in May 2002, when I was producing the finale for *Survivor: Marquesas.* I wanted to do the finale in Manhattan and thought the Trump Wollman skating rink would be the perfect location. Its backdrop of the skyline at night is beautiful and iconic. Our show was to be live from the rink, and with less than two minutes to air I climbed onto the stage and addressed the five thousand fans and guests in attendance. Sitting right there in the front row was Donald Trump himself. I thanked him profusely for allowing us to use the rink and reminded the audience that the naming of the rink had come as a result of his being the only person in Manhattan who was able to figure out a way to get the thing built.

It's a great story, so I told it then and there. Donald Trump had watched the rink flounder for years from his penthouse at Trump Tower, and he was sick of his kids constantly asking him, "Dad, when will the rink be finished so we can go skating?" So he went to battle with Mayor Ed Koch, claiming that the city had totally screwed up the project and that he could finish it in about three months, under budget. In response, Mayor Koch held a press conference where he laughed at this idea. What the mayor did not know was that Trump knew exactly what he was doing. He'd already called the developer of the Montreal Canadians' ice hockey rink and asked for a meeting. The man who built the rink explained that the reason the city was having difficulty maintaining a smooth ice surface on its rink was because they were using refrigeration as opposed to simply using rubber hoses and water. What the city could not achieve in six years, Trump achieved in three and a half months. And as part of his deal, he garnered naming and concession rights forever.

After telling the story, I walked offstage, and with seconds to air, Donald Trump intercepted me and told me he loved *Survivor* and that we should do something together sometime. Fast-forward to later that year. I was now on location in Brazil for our next season. I was at an amazing point in my career. I had already finished fifteen of these very remote, jungle-type shows. We'd already had a cameraman bitten on the hand by a river piranha when he reached into the river for a dropped lens. Every night when heading to tribal council we had to maneuver around the thirty or so crocodiles on the bank as we pulled our boats onto shore. Jaguars were circling our tents at night. One night I was sitting in the jungle thinking there must be some way to spend part of my year back in America, in relative safety. Just as I had that thought, I turned and saw what looked to be millions of insects devouring a carcass. And it popped into my mind right then and there . . . New York City. Where most of the people who live on that small island can't even get a cup of coffee without bumping into somebody in line. It struck me just then as the perfect setting for a competitive, unscripted drama.

And what was it that everyone in New York wanted? They wanted jobs, and they wanted to be rich. And so that evening in December 2002, in the Amazon jungles, the idea for *The Apprentice* was born. The show would be a thirteen-week, televised job interview, but instead of using résumés and interviews the candidates would divide into teams and take on real-world business tasks. The eventual winner would be granted the job opportunity of a lifetime. The only question was whether I could find someone who represented the qualities of entrepreneurship in an iconic way. Someone tough, respected, daring. Someone to possibly helm the show. Who was that no-nonsense businessman who would resonate perfectly with the candidates and with an American audience? I was immediately taken back to that night at Wollman Rink when Donald Trump said he would like to work with me. I thought, *This is meant to be.*

I came back to America and started to get my head around the format for this new business show. I had to go to New York to do some *Survivor* business and thought I'd use that time to reach out to Donald. It was mid-February 2003. I called his office as soon as I landed, hoping to arrange a meeting. I hadn't finalized my pitch just yet but thought I'd have a day or so to think things through. What I hadn't counted on was that Donald Trump was a take-charge guy. When he set his mind on something, he was on it. Right away. He got on the phone and said, "Where are you?" I told him I was in the car leaving LaGuardia. He said, "Come on over. Just tell the doorman, and he'll send you right up."

I thought, *So much for working on my pitch.* I could have put off the meeting, but I didn't want to lose the momentum, even if I wasn't fully prepared. It was now or never. Either I knew the project from top to bottom and believed in it, or I didn't. Before we got started, Donald told me about the kind of reality show everybody was telling him he should do—an *Osbournes*-style show, where the cameras would follow him around as he brushed his teeth and his world-famous hair. He wasn't interested in that, so I walked him through my concept. He loved it. He thought it was very tough and very Trump, and he agreed to do it right then and there. We shook hands on it. That's how Donald Trump does business. He's very instinctual, decisive. He's willing to bet on you as a partner if he believes you have the ability to deliver, and as we left he told his assistant to contact his agent to finalize the deal.

I walked out of the office in a great mood, but that changed soon enough. I got a phone call from Trump's agent, who wasn't too happy. He said, "I wish you would have called me first. As Donald's agent, I should be hearing these ideas before him."

My heart sank. Now I had to repitch the agent—over the phone. The guy was already against the idea, and he hadn't even heard it yet, but I had no choice. I went into my pitch. When I was done, I thought I'd done a better job of it than I had in my face-to-face meeting with Donald, but the agent had a different take. There was a long, uncomfortable silence, and then the agent said, "I don't think that'll work."

This was a distressing development. I knew I could walk back into Donald's office and explain the situation and that there was a good chance we could salvage the deal. But at the same time I thought Donald might start second-guessing himself on the back of his agent's negative opinion. I didn't know Donald at that point, so I had no idea how he would take the news, but he'd certainly seemed like a stand-up guy when we'd shaken hands, and he seemed very enthusiastic about the show. So I went back to his office. He looked up from his desk, smiled, and said, "So it's all worked out, right?"

I said, "Not exactly. There's a problem." Then I explained the problem. When I was through, he did something I might have expected all along. It was so Trump. I hadn't known Donald going into the initial meetings, but now I felt as if I knew him very well. He called in his assistant and asked her to take a note to the agent. It said, "You're fired."

It sealed the deal and suggested a signature line that would soon echo across the country—but it also told me everything I needed to know about what it takes to succeed. And everything I needed to know about my new partner. When Donald Trump gives his word, he keeps it. He had shaken my hand and looked me in the eye, and as far as he was concerned we were in business together. It was a done deal. All he wanted from his agent was some help with the

174

paperwork. He'd made his decision and followed his gut, and nothing was going to get in his way. And he was right. *The Apprentice* became the number one show in the country, and after eight seasons we're still going strong.

Every time I'm on the set, I think how unlikely a partnership it is. Me and Donald Trump. For a naturalized American who once sat on Venice Beach selling T-shirts and reading *The Art of the Deal,* wondering if I would ever make it, to being partners on *The Apprentice*—it's almost magical. It's the magic of America, built on a handshake.

NINE

BUSINESS AS UNUSUAL

Unless a man undertakes more than he can possibly do, he
will never do all that he can.

—HENRY DRUMMOND

Timing is everything.

When I first joined the Trump Organization, it was a great time
to be a real estate developer—not only in New York but all across the
country and in overseas markets as well. Financing was so readily
available that we were able to purchase, develop, manage, and brand a
number of properties around the world, so we had a steady stream of
projects in various stages of the development cycle. Basically, if we
could find an architect to design what we wanted and if we could per-
suade the local municipality to grant us the desired zoning, there was
a very good chance we could get our project built. Our batting average
during this period, measured by our number of hits divided by our
overall plate appearances, was pretty darn good.

One of our architects in Dubai summed it up best. "In today's environment," he said, "the only things holding developers back are gravity and imagination." Indeed, there was a feeling among us developers
that the sky was the limit, but times have changed. Rather quickly.
That's the way it goes in business. What's up one day is down the next.
Opportunities that seem wide open one year are all but closed soon

enough, and it's left to the market leaders to regroup, retrench, and reimagine their businesses if they hope to maintain their edge and remain relevant in the new economy.

More often than not, that edge stays with companies agile enough to respond to such sudden shifts in the marketplace. At the Trump Organization, this meant an overall rethinking of our core business strategy. Even though we still regard ourselves as a real estate development firm, the term *real estate developer* has become a bit of an oxymoron in our sluggish economy, and it was clear to all of us that we needed to be willing to take off our hard hats and make room in our closet for a few new styles. No one is developing new urban towers in this climate, as construction financing has essentially disappeared, so we reconsidered our options. We could cling to our background as developers and waste a lot of energy and resources searching for the funding to get new projects off the ground—business as usual. Or we could reassess our basic model and discover new ways to utilize our unique resources and capabilities in an environment where nothing new was getting built—business as *unusual*.

Happily, we chose the latter, and it's been an interesting shift, one that stands in contrast to our response to the recession that nearly capsized our industry more than fifteen years earlier. Here, the constant has been that we're still making deals, even as the tone and tenor of those deals have changed. One of the most noticeable changes to our overall game plan has been our approach to the hotel business, where we've found some incredible opportunities. The trend in the hotel industry in recent years has been for developers to affiliate with non–real estate brands such as Nobu and Armani, in the hope that the partnership might yield some interesting benefits to the customer experience. In theory, I suppose there might have been something to this line of thinking—but in practice it usually turned out to be an ill-considered mess. At The Trump Organization, we looked on with bemusement at some of the odd pairings, because they seemed to be built on little more than high hopes, general brand recognition, and a smooth PowerPoint presentation. Some of the newly formed "hotel management" companies had no background in the hospitality industry, yet they somehow managed to convince developers that their brands and skills would translate well into the hotel business.

Inevitably, something was lost in the translation. For the most part, these brands didn't understand the hotel management and development business. They didn't understand how to program the right ratio of conference and meeting space to rooms. Or how to design the back-of-house space. Or how to set up and manage a reservations system, or how to hire and train staff in advance of opening, and on and on. They were new to the industry and out of their depth, which would have been fine if all they were doing was lending their name and the strength of their brand to the partnership, but very often the ventures called on their management experience as well—management experience that wasn't directly relevant. People seemed to buy into this flawed model: property owners, licensees, transient guests . . . For a while, in a thriving economy, it was possible for some of the deals to work, but as the market grew tighter and more competitive the inexperience of some of the new management teams became glaringly apparent.

Now, it appears, the pendulum has swung to where many developers are having serious second thoughts about doing business with flags that don't add any tangible and quantifiable value to their projects. *Flag* is an industry term for a hotel brand, and these days I spend a good deal of my time identifying developers who have suddenly become disillusioned with one-off flags and are looking instead to partner with an organization with the infrastructure in place to drive a property's success; from construction to management, from marketing to reservations. The good news is that while I'm out looking for these developers—waving the Trump flag!—they're out looking for me. Objectively, the Trump Organization is one of the few "brand-name" real estate companies with a depth of experience in the development, operations, marketing, and selling of hotel, golf, commercial, and residential properties.

I'm like my dad, I guess, when it comes to singing the praises of our projects and properties. Of late, one of my primary initiatives at the Trump Organization has been to spearhead our hospitality-driven projects, which are now grouped within our Trump Hotel Collection division. Working together with my brothers, Don and Eric, it's been my biggest area of concentration since signing on. (Our joint effort is even reflected in our hotel company's slogan: "The next generation of Trump.") Through our hotel management company, we're currently gearing up to manage projects in Waikiki and in Manhattan's fashionable SoHo district to complement our signature properties in New York, Chicago, and Las Vegas. In future years, we'll be up and running in Toronto, Panama, Scotland, Dubai, the Dominican Republic, and other business and vacation destinations all over the world.

A fundamental objective of our hotel division is to ensure that each new property positively reinforces the Trump "brand," which has come to represent the highest caliber of luxury and excellence, in our hotels, condominiums, and golf clubs. When we work with a local developer to manage a hotel, we're not only planning an outstanding new resort or urban facility and generating a strong new revenue stream; we're also building and extending our brand. That's something we pay close attention to, and I'm betting it will occupy more and more of our time going forward.

So far, the downturn in the economy has worked out just fine for us. Typically, it's easiest to grow a hotel portfolio in a hot market; however, in today's climate, the lack of available financing and the general decrease in travel spending have placed a number of new or half-built hotel projects on hold. With few new hotels being built, we look to team up with disillusioned developers to rebrand and reposition their existing hotel properties. Part of our pitch is that, as developers ourselves, we understand their particular needs and sensitivities and will work with them to achieve their goals. What that means for us is an opportunity to draw on our unique skill set and proven track record to rescue deals from the newly minted management companies and rebrand and reposition the properties to the owners' satisfaction. We expect to see more and more of these types of deals in the months ahead as more and more failing assets appear in need of rebranding.

Another primary focus of my organization these days has been looking for distressed properties that might be available for purchase at a steeply discounted price. In a down economy, there are always great bargains to be had for investors with resources and vision—and perhaps the stomach (and balance sheet!) to carry an asset through a prolonged downturn. Such deals can be tricky from a timing perspective, since you want to buy at or near the bottom of the market, but we're constantly on the lookout for the right opportunity. In this way we've managed to purchase two world-class golf courses, just in the past year, and we expect to find opportunities in the New York City commercial office market in the near future. When we do, we'll be ready to move on projects that are partially built or completed but have fallen into foreclosure or bankruptcy, or have run into some difficulty or other. Yes, we're able to do a deal at an attractive price, but we're also helping investors or lenders get out of a commitment that no longer makes sense for them—maybe not at the terms they envisioned going in but at the prevailing market rate.

In recent months, we've seen the failure of quite a few condominium developments, wiping out the developers of these projects and leaving the banks that financed them in possession of buildings that they don't have the time or the experience to manage or sell. That's been a particular area of windfall opportunity for us, because we're fortunate enough to be in a great cash position. We are constantly meeting with these bankers, looking to acquire properties that they have wound up in possession of. There's not a whole lot of competition for these distressed properties, and banks are more willing to make discounted deals than the desperate developers who are still hanging on and hoping for an upturn. At the end of the day, banks don't want to be stuck with a portfolio of properties. They have no interest in being in the development or asset management business, but we certainly do.

After all, it's one of our strengths.

If you're like me, you've probably read dozens of business books talking up the benefits of going against the grain. Of zigging when everyone else is zagging. Of trying a new approach that runs counter to the market and to conventional wisdom. I wrote about this earlier, in a different context, but in a way I think the strategy is somewhat oversold, so I'll avoid the temptation to offer more of the same. It might be easy to dismiss this instance of the Trump Organization going its own way and doing what it can to buck a downward trend as an example of zigging in a zagging economy. But there's more to it than that. We haven't succeeded in redirecting our business because we've taken a contrarian view; we've succeeded because we're nimble enough to respond to changing market conditions. Being ahead of the curve is sometimes better than building a new road, it turns out. In the end, it simply comes down to being in a position to respond forcefully, as has been the case here. With cash on hand, we've recast ourselves as buyers in a marketplace of sellers because we're in a position to do so—and because doing so provides the best opportunities available to us in the current climate.

An explanation for our favorable cash position is in order. Years ago, my father predicted the current market downturn. We discussed it as a family and agreed that real estate prices were grossly inflated. Rather than continue to acquire real estate and borrow large sums to finance the construction of new developments, we grew our branding, licensing, and management models to eliminate some of those risks. We used Trump International Hotel Tower in New York as the flagship for our newly christened Trump Hotel Collection and meticulously assembled the infrastructure needed for a scalable hotel management company. Most of the expertise we needed to run the operation was already in-house, in areas such as construction management and sales and marketing, so we looked to team with other developers and license our name *and* our know-how and management services to build our collection of assets.

Realize, hotel management companies generally don't own the assets they manage. They don't build the properties either. They simply receive a lucrative, incentive-driven fee for their services. For example, Four Seasons and Ritz-Carlton are not ownership-based hotel companies; they are primarily for-fee managers. Under this model, we could be conservative with our cash, at a time when other developers were not, which allowed us to remain whole and viable when the market turned. We were able to keep money coming into the company coffers through our management and licensing deals, without any significant risk to our bottom line. By bucking the trend and drawing on our strengths and resources, we redirected our company in such a way that we were well positioned for a difficult economy.

If you'd asked me when I started at the Trump Organization what my focus would be in five years, I would have said without hesitation that I'd be building new towers and developing new properties. That was my vision coming in, and it would be my vision going forward. Or so I thought. Ask my father or my brothers, and they would likely have said the same thing. We would never have guessed that we'd be looking to work with other developers to manage and rebrand their ill-positioned projects or that we'd be seeking to acquire them outright from struggling banks—because back then, of course, developers and banks were on top of the world. My passion was, and remains, development and construction. Indeed, that's *our* passion as a company. We know how to build and how to create a whole lot of value in the process. But why build new product when you can buy a revenue-generating building for far less than the cost of construction? It doesn't make sense for us to build right now, so the thing to do is to play the hand we've been dealt. Not to zig while everyone else zags, necessarily, but to learn from all that zigging and zagging and apply those lessons to our bottom line. To take what the market gives us and respond effectively. And, be prepared to change our emphasis yet again in the coming years, when the development pendulum swings back and it will make sense for us to start building again.

What I've never questioned, as my father's prediction of a looming recession began to come true, was the underlying strength of the Trump name. As I said, it's one of our chief assets, but it took having to tough it out in a terrible economy for me to recognize the intangible value of what my father had built—of what we will continue to build together as a family.

EXTENDING THE REACH

Here's an odd picture: my father, onstage at the 2005 Emmy Awards, singing the theme song from *Green Acres* with the actress Megan Mullally. Even odder, he was wearing a straw hat and overalls and holding a pitchfork. It was an absurdly funny scene—one for which our international partners would have had absolutely no frame of reference. What in the world was Donald Trump, one of the world's leading real estate developers, doing onstage in a musical comedy skit?

I had no answer. All I could do was think, This is not normal. It was entertaining but not normal. My father's not normal. *We* are not normal. This wasn't at all how things were supposed to go in the typically staid world of business, but then I guessed this just meant we weren't typically staid businesspeople. Well, we were and we weren't. We were making deals, but at the same time we were making a name for ourselves—a name that would carry a certain amount of weight and announce our interests long before we even had a chance to weigh in for ourselves.

Don't misunderstand, it was a harmless, funny sketch, and I loved watching my father do his thing—he was such a ham!—but at the same time it was such a weirdly surreal moment. I caught myself wondering how I might describe it to any of our overseas associates, who might not have had such a nuanced appreciation for how my father had positioned himself here at home at the intersection of business and popular culture.

Early on in his career, my father recognized a unique opportunity to harness the power of the media and use it to his professional advantage. Good for him, right? He cultivated his public image in such a way that the Trump name would come to stand for excellence, luxury, and the very highest standards. Good for business, right? He himself took on the same characteristics, because he knew that people wouldn't distinguish between his business and his persona.

My father is a very smart guy, but even he couldn't have seen all of this attention coming his way. He didn't set out to be a media personality. Being famous wasn't one of his goals. Rich, maybe. But famous? Not so much. He'd set out to be a successful developer, just as his father had been before him, and he surely was. But the more successful he became, the more he started to interact with the press, the more he realized his growing celebrity was an asset waiting to happen. He projected a winning, vibrant, upmarket persona, and people seemed to respond to it in a big-time way. And it fit hand in hand with the impression he wanted people to take from his properties. A positive public image, he began to realize, would help promote his buildings and enhance his reputation as an entrepreneur. He came to represent a lavish lifestyle and a brash, bold way of doing business that quickly became the American ideal.

Uniquely positioned as a celebrity businessman, my father was given great media exposure, so he made sure to hold up his end. He lived large. He threw legendary parties at Mar-a-Lago and attended the fabulous parties of others. He bought an airline—the Eastern Shuttle, which he renamed the Trump Shuttle. He bought a football team—the New Jersey Generals, of the upstart United States Football League. He acquired and refurbished a storied yacht—renamed the *Trump Princess*, for yours truly. He wrote a book. He took over a city landmark and rescued it from oblivion. Then he did it again. And again. When my parents' marriage broke up, he became New York City's most eligible bachelor, and his comings and goings were front-page fodder for the tabloids.

At one point he looked up and realized he had become a brand—a commodity, even. Just like one of his buildings or resort properties. The Trump name had come to represent one of his biggest assets as a businessman. It was bigger than any one deal, because it transcended every deal. It got to where he could launch a development in the middle of Manhattan and another in the middle of nowhere, and both projects would make international news. After all, *he* was news. With each new building, he told another chapter of *his* story. Every successful venture offered an exclamation point to every previous venture and speculation about the ventures still to come. Without really intending to do so, my father had become a celebrity, and his celebrity couldn't help but enhance the Trump brand. Other developers spent millions of dollars trying to gain exposure for their projects, while the Trump Organization spent virtually nothing. Actually, we hardly ever advertise our properties—at least not in a traditional sense. Why buy an ad in a magazine when we can grant an interview to that same publication and possibly land a cover story? That's the kind of exposure no amount of advertising dollars can buy.

One of the best examples of my father's ability to grow his success as a developer through the media is *The Apprentice*, his hit reality show on NBC. In hindsight, my father's decision to do a prime-time network show might seem like a no-brainer, but at the time it was no sure thing. As reality television came of age, my father kept fielding requests from this or that producer, looking to follow him around with their cameras, but he always turned down their proposals because they didn't really offer him a substantive opportunity. He didn't need the money. He didn't need the attention. And he didn't need to put himself up for public inspection in a vehicle that might leave him open for scrutiny or ridicule.

Then Mark Burnett came calling. Mark was the wildly successful producer of *Survivor*, a reality show that in many ways redefined the genre. In a short time, he'd made a name for himself as the top guy in his field. His shows had a signature look, a signature style. It's not just that his shows tended to be successful, but they stood apart in terms of quality and appeal. They featured a trademark sense of high drama, complete with cliff-hanger endings and all kinds of compelling, tension-filled reasons for people at home to tune in week after week. The two of them met while Mark was in New York shooting a *Survivor* finale. It's a story Mark shared just before this chapter, so I won't repeat it here except to say that he and my father got together on an idea for a business show that would basically be one long job interview. Contestants would vie for a job at my father's company, and my father would get to "hire" or "fire" them as he saw fit.

Everybody in my father's circle told him to steer clear. His agent. His friends. His closest advisers. Even his kids. No business show had ever done well in prime time. I didn't understand why my father would risk tarnishing his hard-won image with a poorly received television show. But my father saw things a little differently. For one thing, he liked Mark Burnett—and he believed in him. He trusted Mark to be a good caretaker of his public image. He trusted his instincts, too. If a hit-making producer like Mark Burnett thought he could get ratings with a business concept, my father was inclined to agree with him. Primarily, though, my father thought it'd be fun. In the end, that was really his first and last argument for agreeing to lend his name and his time to the effort. When I pulled him aside to ask him what, exactly, he'd be doing on the show, he said, "Ranting and raving like a lunatic." Of course, there'd be more to it than that, but he had a sense of humor about himself and a realistic sense of how he fit into this particular enterprise.

There again, my father was smarter than the rest of us—but not *that* smart. Even he couldn't have predicted the enormous success of *The Apprentice*. It was the number one show on television in its first season, and it's become one of NBC's most valuable franchises. My father's celebrity was enhanced exponentially—and along with it, the Trump name shone brighter than ever before. The success of the show paved the way for me and my brother Don to develop public personas of our own, with prominent roles on the spin-off, *Celebrity Apprentice.*

My father's triumph in this arena is particularly notable when you do a quick head count of all the CEOs who've tried to launch business shows of their own since *The Apprentice* debuted in 2003—from Mark Cuban's *The Benefactor* to Richard Branson's *The Rebel Billionaire* and even on to Martha Stewart's softer version of *The Apprentice.* Clearly, the skeptics and naysayers were right to suggest that it's impossible to succeed with a reality business show in prime time—unless you happen to be Donald Trump.

Fundamentally, my father understands how to entertain people. It's at the core of almost everything he does. That's why he's been successful in areas where other businessmen have been somewhat less so. He understands what buyers of luxury real estate want out of the transaction, what television viewers want from a reality host, even what Emmy audiences want from their awards show. He delivers because he delivers himself.

At the Trump Organization and around our family dinner table, we're all thrilled by the unbelievable run of *The Apprentice* and endlessly appreciative of the opportunities the show has brought to our company, but we also understand the ephemeral nature of hit television shows. This was never more apparent to my father than it was during a conversation he had with *Saturday Night Live* producer Lorne Michaels. Early on in his *Apprentice* run, my father admitted that even though NBC executives were ecstatic with the ratings, he was trying not to let the show's success go to his head.

He said, "I know one day they'll call me and say, 'You're fired, Donald' "—echoing the signature catchphrase he'd made famous on the show.

"No," corrected Lorne, a savvy television veteran. "They won't even call."

The Trump Organization was already the world's most recognized development company before the show, but *The Apprentice* has raised our visibility as a family and as a development company to a whole new level. That's been especially true for Don and me. By appearing on my father's show—now on a regular basis on *Celebrity Apprentice*—my brother and I have become almost instant celebrities. We'd always been well known, as my father's two oldest children and in my case as a fleetingly successful model, but now we were being recognized as accomplished, forthright young professionals in our own right—and key players on my father's team. The exposure we've received on the show has had an immediate impact at the Trump Organization, where we were suddenly slotted in as integral members of the management team. That is, we were suddenly slotted into these roles as far as the public knew; in fact, we'd held those positions all along, but in our own, low-key way. This public change of face would have surely taken place over time, but the television show put us on an accelerated schedule, and it put the development community on notice that we had our father's ear—and his trust.

Almost overnight, it seemed, Don and I were cast as high-profile emissaries for my father's company, and the Trump "brand" seemed to transition in real estate and media circles into more of a family brand. Because of our roles on the show, people were suddenly inclined to take us more seriously than they might have otherwise. This was particularly noticeable overseas, once *The Apprentice* franchise was syndicated in more than one hundred countries, from Mexico to Malaysia to Mongolia. As a result, when I travel to work on a deal, it becomes a big story. Forget the deal itself—the mere fact of our interest in a region or a particular property is now considered newsworthy in some parts of the world.

Sometimes, my newfound celebrity can get in the way of whatever deal I'm negotiating, but for the most part it tends to offer an enormous competitive advantage. Once, when we were on a trip to Istanbul to announce our partnership on a two-tower residential and office complex with the Dogan Group, Turkey's preeminent conglomerate, the show factored in to our launch in an unexpected way. The purpose of the trip was to announce the project at a party I was cohosting with the Dogan family, but the party ended up receiving far more attention than our team could have anticipated. More than thirty Turkish newspapers received credentials to attend, and my photo was plastered on front pages all across the country the next morning—all because of my suddenly high-profile role on *Celebrity Apprentice*. Our partners at the Dogan Group were certainly pleased at the extra attention, because there's no way anyone could have afforded that kind of publicity with a typical ad budget.

The same type of greeting awaited me on a recent trip to Israel, only here I was merely chasing down a number of potential leads. There was no one percolating deal demanding to be put on our front burners. Still, my arrival for what was essentially a fact-finding mission generated a tremendous amount of press, and by the time I'd returned to my office back home I'd heard from half the developers in Israel with proposals for joint ventures or development projects they hoped would fit our luxury criteria—again, all on the back of this swirl of media attention.

There's been no escaping the scope and reach of *The Apprentice*—even when some countries were still playing catch-up and broadcasting shows from our first few seasons while we were showing our eighth or ninth season back home. This was the case on a trip to Dubai with Andy Litinsky, the Harvard graduate who was one of the contestants during the show's second season. Andy didn't end up winning that year—my father had to fire him for doing a poor job as project manager late in the season—but we were impressed by his abilities and his drive to succeed. In fact, we liked Andy so much that we ended up hiring him after taping the last show. He worked under me and Donnie for several years in real estate before moving to Los Angeles to head up Trump Productions, where he's done an amazing job producing television programs such as MTV's *Pageant Place* and *The Girls of Hedsor Hall.*

But that's getting ahead of the story—or behind, as our fans in Dubai would soon discover. You see, we'd gone to Dubai to meet with Nakheel, the Emirates' largest developer. Whenever we returned to our hotel after a long day of meetings, or went out for meals, we were mobbed by hundreds of *Apprentice* fans. The show was the country's top-rated program, but those people weren't turning out to see me or my brother. Dubai television was running a few seasons behind, and audiences had yet to see us on the show. In fact, they were still in the middle of Andy's season during our visit, and he had yet to be eliminated. The irony in our timing was that when the locals saw Andy traveling with us, they immediately assumed he must have been the winner. Some people were actually upset, because they'd invested all that time in watching the first several episodes and thought we'd spoiled the balance of the season for them by revealing Andy as the next "Apprentice." We had to keep explaining to all these fans that they shouldn't read too much into Andy's presence, since we were already in preproduction on our seventh season, but no matter how much we tried to convince them otherwise, everyone believed the trip to Dubai was part of Andy's prize for winning season two.

The fuss and attention certainly did wonders for Andy's ego, but it also impressed our friends at Nakheel. The three of us moved about like rock stars, and it didn't hurt that Andy was our front man for this trip. Don and I certainly didn't care that he had the spotlight. What counted was that the show had done some important advance work for us, and that's been the case on countless occasions. In a world obsessed with branding and celebrity, our partners are very impressed to see this kind of validation of their decision to work with the Trump brand. They love the fanfare and the positive spillover to our joint efforts. And they love that it's unique. Nobody freaks out when a high-ranking executive from Related Companies or Four Seasons visits one of their development projects. No matter how successful or how vast their portfolio of properties, real estate developers and hotel operators aren't generally regarded as celebrities—with one exception.

Whether it's in Dubai, in Istanbul, or at home in Manhattan, the public relations boost we receive from *The Apprentice,* and lately from our various other appearances and entertainment projects, has given us a quantifiable advantage over our competitors. The Corcoran Group, New York City's biggest real estate agency, recently concluded a study that determined that the Trump "brand" on a Manhattan building created a 35 percent increase in value relative to our competition. That's huge. And the strength of our brand is paying even greater dividends overseas. Our introductory sales price at our project in Panama, just to cite one example, was more than three times the previous highs in that market. Clearly, through our worldwide media exposure, we've created tremendous value, at virtually no cost. Alongside a commitment to luxury and uncompromising quality, it's been the cornerstone of our business.

The lesson? Well, it wouldn't be reasonable to suggest that young entrepreneurs go out and land their own reality show to raise their public profile or to work it out so they just happen to be born to a media magnet of a dad who's managed to turn the family name into a precious commodity. But there is an important takeaway—namely, that there's tremendous value in staying open to new ideas and opportunities. Keep the core business focused, but look for opportunities in unusual places to reinforce that core. In any business, in any field, it's all too easy to become set in your ways and rest on past accomplishments. The key is to weigh the opportunities all around you and pursue the ones that make the most sense, but you'll never pursue any of them if you're not flexible in your thinking. Don't fall into the trap of listening to conventional thinkers—to the so-called experts who'll try to tell you a business show would never work in prime time. Instead, go with your gut. Do what *feels* right. Be prepared to reinvent yourself, your business, your approach—because you'll need to grow and evolve if you plan to stay relevant over the long run.

THE CONFIDENCE BOOST

Not long ago, I received an e-mail from the CEO of an Indonesian conglomerate. The gentleman explained that he was looking for a company to manage several of his Asian hotels and had been referred to me by a mutual acquaintance at a leading U.S. financial services firm.

Up to that point, the exchange was fairly typical. Indeed, I get messages like that all the time. They're a big part of my job, the entry point, really, for a lot of the deals we end up pursuing. Typically, the e-mails lead to a phone call, and that's when things can get interesting. As the twenty-seven-year-old daughter of the best-known real estate developer in the world, I can usually detect an undercurrent of doubt or suspicion on the part of the caller. More often than not, it's right on the surface. Sometimes it's just beneath. In most of these conversations, there seems to be a long list of unasked questions lining up on the other end of the phone. I can almost feel them, about to bubble forth, or imagine the caller biting his lip, trying not to give them voice or let them up for air.

The questions are always the same: "Didn't you used to be a model?"

Or "I remember watching you on television when you were just a little girl, so how could you possibly know what you're talking about?"

Or "Why do I have to go through *you* in order to get to *him*?"

I've never actually heard this last one, but I know it's there. Waiting for me. I don't think I'll ever hear it, though, because most people don't have the courage to speak their minds in this way—which means that since most of the questions are hardly ever asked, I hardly ever have to answer them. That's just fine with me. I've prepared for them, which is something I always try to do, prepare for every contingency. I have no trouble deflecting them when they do come up, but they usually stay way down on a long list and never reach the top.

On this particular call, the executive held his tongue and managed to keep his concerns to himself. If he even had any concerns. Every now and then my associates don't question my background, I'm happy to report. Every now and then the benefit of the doubt is mine, and nobody judges me or questions my abilities. More and more, these issues are surfacing less and less as I develop a track record and a reputation. It seemed that particular inquiry would come without any preconceived notions of what I could or couldn't do, the assessments or analyses I was or wasn't capable of making, the place I did or did not deserve in my father's company. That was encouraging—and, most welcome. In fact, there was a lot to like about the call, and the broad parameters of the deal the CEO was proposing certainly seemed to warrant a follow-up discussion. So we set up a conference call for a few days later with the CEO and some of his colleagues—also fairly typical for a call such as that one. On the follow-up conference call, I talked about the many hotel projects that the Trump Organization was working on domestically and internationally and then explained what criteria we look for in a developer to work with. The CEO and his colleagues spoke more specifically about their proposed deal. The conversation lasted almost an hour, and in the end both sides were optimistic about the prospect of working together.

So far, so good.

Then it came. The question I knew this guy had been dying to ask. He'd put it off for the longest time, but as we said our good-byes it finally came out. "Ms. Trump," he started in, "I must confess, when our friend first suggested I contact you, I was very confused."

"Why is that?" I said. I suspected I already knew the answer, but I played along.

"I was under the impression that you were only a model," the CEO explained almost sheepishly.

I heard that and thought, Ah-ha! Here we go! Took you long enough!

On my end, that part of the conversation was like pulling teeth; I believed I knew where the Indonesian executive was going, but I wanted to let him finish. On the CEO's end, it was as if he was having his teeth pulled; he knew what he wanted to say, but he wanted to choose his words carefully and be doubly sure he didn't offend me. Nevertheless, he continued with the extraction: "I thought our friend had misunderstood me," he said, "and believed I was looking for someone to make a paid appearance at one of our hotels. But now, after having spoken with you, I can see quite clearly why he gave me your name."

I was momentarily surprised by the comment, but I was happy to hear it just the same. And I said as much. "Thank you," I said. "That's nice to hear."

"It's been a real pleasure," the executive reiterated, "and I look forward to doing business with your company."

And that was that. Nothing terrible or untoward. Nothing unprofessional. Yet some women in my position might have taken exception to the CEO's remark. They might have interpreted it as a backhanded compliment, but I didn't hear it that way at all. It's possible I might have, at some point early in my career, but not any longer. Don't misunderstand, this guy was perfectly pleasant, polite, and appropriate. He was careful to couch his observation in the most politically and socially correct manner, but the underlying assumption of his comment could certainly have come across as offensive. Yet it didn't bother me at all, not even for a split second. Why? Well, I was used to it, for one thing. I have a tough skin, for another—and enough confidence in myself and my abilities not to worry too much about being underestimated or dismissed because of my last name, my youth, or my modeling background. It comes with the territory. Besides, I'd reached the point where I knew I was no lightweight and that I was perfectly capable of separating people from this type of snap judgment.

In business, it's gotten to where I am now able to use my training as my father's apprentice to look at every opportunity through my father's eyes. I don't need to consult with him directly, but I'll think, Dad wouldn't touch this deal. Or, Dad's gonna love this. It colors my approach. That's what a positive and strong mentor influence can do for you. I heard his voice when I was preparing to launch the Ivanka Trump Collection. I would be out on my own with this venture, but at the same time I realized I would never be completely alone. I'd have my father with me. My mother and my brothers, too, but mostly my father. I'd hear his voice in my head, telling me to steer clear or to forge ahead, and know I was moving in the right direction. Or not. Just as I'd heard his voice as a teenager in that body-piercing shop, steering me right before I could make a big mistake.

HYPE AND SUBSTANCE

When I was about nine years old, I stood in my father's office and looked at a framed magazine cover he had on his wall. I remember the moment as if it happened yesterday. The cover featured a picture of my father under the headline "Donald Trump: What's Behind the Hype?" It was typical of a lot of the coverage he used to get in those days, but that was about to change.

The 1980s had been very good for my father and the Trump Organization. He had become the most prominent player in New York real estate. But the markets stalled in the early 1990s, and business in general lost some momentum. A lot of developers faltered, due to the lousy economy, but my father placed a lot of the blame for his company's struggles on himself. Looking back, he believes he lost his focus. It didn't help, of course, that the country was up against it, but my father knew that if he had been on his game he would have seen the crisis coming. As it was, he believed the dedication, single-minded sense of ambition, and purpose that had characterized the first phase of his career had seemed to slip away from him. He'd bought into his own hype, he now says, and allowed himself to become distracted by all these sideline pursuits. He read an article in *Business Week* beneath the headline "Everything Trump Touches Turns to Gold" and generally started to believe it.

In the fallout of the savings and loan scandal of the late 1980s, the real estate market crumbled, helping to push our entire economy into a serious recession. The Trump Organization, like most developers, was caught off guard. All of a sudden, banks such as Chase, Citicorp, and Bankers Trust started calling in their loans, demanding that my father repay immediately the huge sums they'd made available for new Trump projects.

He soon found himself hundreds of millions in debt, and he was getting beaten up in the press every day. The speculation was that he was through as a developer. Even some of his "friends" were inclined to write him off, but he tried not to lose his perspective. One day during this period, my father was walking down Fifth Avenue with his then wife, Marla, when he came across a homeless man sitting in front of Trump Tower. My father turned to Marla and said, "You know, that guy has 900 million dollars more than me."

I wasn't sure what he meant by this when he told me the story afterward, at least not at first. He was standing in front of a magnificent building with our name on it. How could a homeless man possibly have been in better financial shape than my father?

"At least he doesn't owe any money," my father explained when he saw how confused I looked. "He's got nothing, but I owe 900 million. By my count, that makes him far richer than me."

I was too young to fully grasp the enormity of what the Trump Organization was facing, but for several years the company teetered on the brink of bankruptcy. Yet with just the right mix of stamina, stubbornness, and savvy, my father found his way to the other side of that crisis. Unlike most of his developer friends, he never declared bank-ruptcy, and he didn't merely survive, he emerged stronger than ever. He simply refused to quit. He worked relentlessly to save his empire. He sold his toys. He cut back on expenses. He spent countless hours nego-tiating with bankers and cajoling them to restructure his debts.

I'm sure he took it personally, finding himself in such a steep and sudden hole and reading the negative things some of the newspapers were saying about him, but he wasn't about to let his ego get in the way of his company's survival. In the end, thanks to the hard work and re-siliency of my father and his team, my father was able to reestablish himself and ultimately grow his company to new heights; even though I admire everything my father has accomplished over the years, I'm proudest of his strength during the difficult days of the early 1990s. Of course, my father was hardly the only developer to flirt with disas-ter during this period, but he was one of the few to stage such an ex-traordinary comeback. Many of his competitors couldn't see a way out of their predicaments and ended up liquidating their companies— throwing in the towel. Many of them went bankrupt. To them, quit-ting was easier than fighting. To my father, quitting was out of the question.

His relentless attitude in the face of such dire circumstances goes back to the "gravity and imagination" comment voiced by our archi-tect in Dubai. Here, the weight, or *gravity,* of the problems faced by the Trump Organization might have been enough to shut down the dreams, or *imagination,* of any visionary, but my father would not be considered just any visionary. His imagination and vision would see him through, he determined. Of course, it didn't hurt that he was te-nacious and that there was enough luster already invested in the Trump brand to keep it from tarnishing.

His struggles during that period continue to inspire me, and I have to think there's a great lesson to learn from his tenacity. People tend to give up without much of a fight, in business and in everything else. It doesn't have to carry the weight or gravity of a $900 million debt. It could be $5,000 owed to a credit card company. It could be an unpaid student loan, accruing interest while the borrower has yet to lock down a first job after graduation. It could be a middle manager stuck in a position that doesn't seem to be going anywhere. It could be a student unable to get it together to study for the LSATs. There are roadblocks to our success at every turn, and it's up to each of us to find the resiliency and strength of character to get past them. Instead of calling the credit card company and trying to restructure their debt, some people hide from creditors or declare bankruptcy. Instead of arriving early and working late so they can make a stronger case for promotion, some people simply tap through the hours and hope their mediocre work might continue to go unnoticed. Instead of signing up for a tutoring course or doubling down on time spent studying, some people never take the LSATs and allow their dreams of becoming a lawyer to fall away. My father refused to be one of these people. And now, because of his inspiration, I refuse to be one of these people.

Finding the fortitude needed to achieve long-term success is one of the fundamental challenges facing young people in business. We're blessed to have come of age in a very strong market, but now many of us are struggling for the first time in our careers. The roadblocks that once seemed like speed bumps might now appear insurmountable—but be assured, there's a way around them.

A friend who runs one of the country's largest hedge funds recently told me how frustrated he was with his young employees. "I don't know what the hell to do with people your age," he complained to me one afternoon—as if I were personally responsible for the failings of my generation. "You all came out of school straight into the hottest market in history. None of you know how to look at deals without being overly optimistic. You expect every deal to make you millions of dollars overnight, and when it doesn't happen that way you get frustrated and move on to the next 'big thing.'"

He was right. We *have* been conditioned to expect success—sometimes instantly. Too many of my peers were happy to reap the rewards of a strong market but lack the backbone to survive a recession. They will need that perseverance, however, because markets always change. The key, if you're out to achieve lasting success, is to ride out the busts and to identify and seize the opportunities you'll surely find in the wreckage.

To repeat: timing is everything. Now, when you're just starting out, is the time to build a strong foundation. Be patient, and keep your eyes open for new opportunities. Consider the example of Trump Place, our luxury eight-building development overlooking the Hudson River on Manhattan's West Side. It's a sprawling residential complex that covers nearly twenty city blocks, and it's really quite impressive. Our family's involvement in the property goes all the way back to 1974, when my father first optioned the rights to the land for $10 million. He ended up closing the deal in January 1985 and received his final zoning approvals in December 1992. His initial vision for the West Side project was to build a breathtaking development that would include a massive television studio and the world's tallest building. He faced some legendary and well-chronicled difficulties getting zoning for the project, however, and he also encountered resistance from critics who wanted him to build something on a much smaller scale. There was considerable pressure on the company to abandon the project entirely, but my father wouldn't quit. Instead, he spent decades fighting for the right to develop Trump Place in a manner that he thought was appropriate, one that would maximize the property's value and fulfill his vision. He knew that a parcel of land that large would probably never become available in Manhattan again, and he refused to compromise on either the project's quality or its scale. He was willing to fight for thirty years if that's what it took to see it through—and it ended up taking him just a few years longer than that.

Today, Trump Place is one of Manhattan's unsurpassed luxury

destinations, a development that shows off "the best side of the West Side"—as stated in the collateral materials.

How many young people have the patience and dedication to wait more than thirty years to see a project to fruition? Not many, I'm afraid—but that's the mind-set you'll need to embrace if you hope to achieve lasting success.

TORY BURCH—Fashion designer

ON FOLLOWING YOUR GUT

When I started my company, many people told me not to launch as a retail concept because it was too big a risk. People said I should launch at wholesale and test the waters first because that was the more traditional and safer route.

As the concept was taking shape in my mind, my father encouraged me to be bold and go for it. He was a successful investor and entrepreneur, so I trusted his instincts. He understood what it meant to take risks. He also recognized my passion for design and my deep commitment to making this venture a success. He helped me keep it all in perspective and taught me what having confidence in my vision and following through with focus and determination can do.

Now when people ask me for guidance, I always pass along the same advice: Stay true to your vision, and don't be afraid of taking risks, even when it means going against the grain.

TEN

REACHING OUT, PLUGGING IN

I'm convinced that one of the reasons that I've been
successful is that I've almost always competed against
people who were bigger and stronger but who had less
commitment and desire than I did.

—TED TURNER

A lot of people assume I've learned everything I know about business
from my father. There's no denying he's taught me a lot, but I've also
picked up a lot from my mother—and a great deal more on my own.
I've developed my own style, but I see my parents' influences in how I
set up my days and go about my routines.

That's one of the great things about a career in business. There's
no fixed road map we're all meant to follow. We're free to pick and
choose a path that works, to turn away from what doesn't, and to borrow liberally from mentors and role models who are kind enough to
offer direction along the way. If something works for a while and then
no longer makes sense, you can try something new. If some tactic
turns out to surprise you with a positive outcome, you can go back to
it again and again. Happily, you can't trademark a sound business
strategy or a personal style, so I'm always on the lookout for new

methods to invigorate my approach. I've come to believe that one of
the greatest assets you can have as a young businessperson is an open
mind, and you need to nurture and nourish that type of thinking if
you mean to get and stay ahead. Personal and professional growth and
refinement are not a once-in-a-while sort of effort. They need to be a
constant focus in your life, the foundation of every initiative and strategy you'll undertake, or you'll fall out of step and allow your competitors to pass you by.

The first thing I do every morning, right after scanning my Black-
Berry, is catch up on what's going on in the world. I'll usually watch
CNBC's *Squawk Box* as I get ready for work, but to my thinking the
single best way to tap into the news and developments of the day is to
read the newspaper. Unfortunately, I'm very nearly alone in this among
my generation. I've covered this already, I know, but it bears repeating.
Most of my peers stay connected to the world through a variety of
other means, most of them electronic, but I still reach for my morning
paper. There's nothing like it for an in-depth look at the markets and
market makers I need to consider as I go about my business. I'll admit,
Google Reader is slowly luring me in, but I still love the print product.
I suspect I always will. If I'm traveling, I'll make a point to read the
local paper, too. I also read a variety of trade and special-interest publications, such as *Crain's* and *Women's Wear Daily*. If there's time, I
might even visit some of the more influential Web sites, such as The
Huffington Post, The Drudge Report, and Observer.com—whatever I
can find to help me keep on top of the news and on top of my game.

PUT IT IN WRITING

As I read, I make little notes to myself. Bulletins, reminders, prospects . . . whatever comes to mind. Most significantly, I'll write down
the names of people who are making moves relevant to my businesses,
shaking things up in an admirable way, or generally going about their
careers in ways I find inspiring or illuminating. Maybe I'll just make a

note of someone I should make an effort to know. It could be a developer who's announced a new project, a real estate agent who just made a record sale on a town house, or a fashion designer with a hot new collection. Some days the list of names can get pretty long, and when I'm done I'll check those people out online. (Thank you, Google!) Other days I might not be inspired to write down a single name. When I do make the effort, I'll usually send a brief, handwritten note, introducing myself and explaining that I've been following that person's career. Typically, I express my admiration, or I extend my congratulations if that's appropriate—my version of a shout-out, I guess.

My thinking here is basic: if I'm inspired by somebody, I'll do well to let him or her know about it. I do this on the theory that you never know how people will respond, but chances are it might lead to a positive connection. I put myself in their shoes and think how validating it would feel—how nice!—to hear from someone with a thoughtful, appreciative comment about something I'm working on. It's not that I expect those people to acknowledge my correspondence, but many have, so there's been a real and enduring benefit to the effort. Realize, there's no end game to it, even though there's very often a side benefit, and that's the reason it's been such an effective practice for me. It's genuine. It comes from a positive place, and it costs me nothing more than a few minutes of my time and the price of a stamp. As it happens, the overriding fringe benefit is the chance to forge a relationship with someone doing interesting and innovative work, someone who may or may not turn out to be a valuable contact. But at the moment it's really just a gesture, to let the person on the receiving end know that someone admires and appreciates what they're doing. That's all. It's cold calling of a kind, only not in the sense that direct marketers use the term. It's just me, reaching out as an individual to someone I want to know or get to know better.

I've found this to be an incredibly valuable but surprisingly underutilized way to improve your network of contacts. A handwritten note can be such a powerful tool, especially when it's set against the heat and haste of how most people communicate these days. It's one of the great habits I picked up from my father. These days it seems that the handwritten personalized note has gone the way of the rotary telephone, but I believe the antiquated charm makes these notes stand out all the more. Think about it: with e-mails and instant messaging and Facebook and Twitter, we're running out of reasons to actually put pen to paper. We've put all these shortcuts into place, and at the same time we've built virtual walls around what we do; taken together, the new landscape gets in the way of any kind of substantive interaction and focused communication.

It puts a lot of unnecessary distance between us, don't you think? I certainly do, and my idea with these unexpected notes is to turn back the clock a little and maybe catch someone of influence by surprise. Twenty years ago, when I watched my mother send out her handwritten thank-you notes on her lovely embossed stationery, it was a nice touch. Yet in some ways, it was what was expected of you, to acknowledge an invitation or a lunch meeting or a kindness in an Emily Post–type way. Now, though, this type of communication stands out. People really respond to it. It's not like a phone call or an e-mail. It's far more intimate, far more personal, because we've gotten out of the habit.

Recently, I got a great tip from Robert Toll, the CEO of Toll Brothers, one of the most successful builders of luxury homes in the country. We'd gotten together to discuss a project, and I followed up with a note thanking him for taking the time to visit our office. At the same time, Bob was following up with a note of his own, only his letter blew mine right out of the water. It was incredible—three pages long! Typically, I'll just write a few sentences. Anything more, and my short attention span kicks in! My handwriting isn't great and I'm a terrible speller, and I write so many of these missives that I can't spend too much time on any one note in particular.

Bob's letter made such an impression that I brought it up the next time I saw him. I said, "Bob, thank you so much for the lovely note, but how the hell did you find the time to write three full pages? You're one of the busiest developers in America!"

He laughed, and then he let me in on his secret. He said, "It's funny that you ask, Ivanka. I just got this new software program, and I was trying it out. You're the first person who's said something about it."

I thanked Bob for his candor and told him how much I appreciated his note and our visit. Then I went out and got a copy of the software—because, after all, I'm only too happy to borrow someone else's bright idea and make it my own. It turned out to be one of the best timesaving moves I ever made. What an ingenious creation! I had to have one of the tech guys in the office help me install it, but it was worth the extra effort. Essentially, you write out every letter in the alphabet, in lowercase and uppercase, and then upload the writing sample. The software registers your handwriting, along with every conceivable punctuation mark. You can also input your signature and any other personal touches you might want to toss into the mix. After that, it's just like any other font. Instead of choosing Times New Roman or Arial or some other typeface for your documents, you can select the Handwriting font. Now I can dictate all my notes or type them on my laptop or my BlackBerry when I'm traveling—and print them out, in ink, on my personalized stationery. In my own handwriting! It's such a godsend—and no one can tell the difference! True enough, I probably shouldn't spread the word so freely about this lovely invention, because I wouldn't want this nice personal touch to become just as impersonal as all our other forms of correspondence. But why not co-opt technology for a change and put it to work *for* us instead of continuing to be co-opted by it?

One of the most rewarding "cold calls" I ever made was to the Mexican billionaire Carlos Slim Helú, who had just made headlines by bailing out *The New York Times* with a $250 million loan. Most Americans had never heard of him before his involvement with the *Times,* but the man known as "the Mexican Warren Buffett" is well known in financial circles as one of the true giants of the twentieth century. *Forbes* magazine dubbed him one of the richest men in the world—so, clearly, this was someone worth knowing. Not for his wealth but for his wealth of experience and the wisdom he had gained in building his fortune. I never expected to hear back from him, but I dashed off a note just the same. (For the record, it was before I picked up that handwriting software, so I *really* put pen to paper on that one.) I'd known Carlos Slim as a leader in Mexican real estate development, even though he'd made his fortune in telecommunications, but his dramatic rescue of the *Times* seemed like the perfect opportunity to make a connection. The note was little more than a fan letter. In it I told Carlos Slim that I'd been following his career, that I thought he was brilliant, and that I would be honored to meet with him if he ever had time on a visit to New York.

And that was that. I sent it off never expecting to hear back, but about a week later I got a call from Carlos Slim's office telling me he was in town and available to meet me at his hotel that night. Naturally, I dropped my other plans and arrived at the designated time. If you have an opportunity to learn from someone like Carlos Slim and don't take advantage of it, it's an opportunity lost. And so, for the next two hours, this kind, visionary business leader graciously shared his thoughts with me on a myriad of topics: the relationship between Mexico and the United States, the future of media, the role of telecommunications in the developing world, trends in the real estate market, and his philosophy on business in general. When I left, I felt as if I'd absorbed as much information in two hours of casual conversation as I had in countless classes at Wharton. It was truly amazing. To this day, I look back on my conversation with Carlos Slim as a career highlight, even though there was no direct or tangible benefit and no deal being considered. It was just a discussion—although, granted, it was a bit of a lopsided exchange.

My father, I should point out, was quite proud when I called him on the walk back from Carlos's hotel to my apartment. I said, "You'll never guess who I just met with." And then I couldn't wait for him to guess, so I told him.

"Wow," he said. "*You* got an audience with Carlos Slim? I guess you really *are* my daughter!"

Quite often, my notes yield more concrete results. Once, I read an article in *The Wall Street Journal* about a foreign developer who was building a massive mixed-use complex in the Middle East. I was impressed with the size and scale of the job and immediately pegged it as a Trump-type project. I looked up the developer's contact information online and called to congratulate him on his efforts to date and to introduce myself. I closed the call by suggesting that we brand his project as a Trump property and manage the on-site hotel. I described to the developer the value we could create for his project, from our construction and design expertise to the premium we would generate on the salable real estate component of the job, and he listened with great interest. The developer had been close to wrapping a deal with another five-star hotel operator, so I flew to London to meet with him the very next day to make my case in person. By the end of the week we'd reached an agreement to partner on the development.

A great many of these "shout-outs" have nothing to do with business. Some are just for fun. Not too long ago, I met the rapper and producer Kanye West at a *Vanity Fair* dinner during the Tribeca Film Festival and I thought I'd follow up with a note. This was no small feat—my assistant had to get past six or seven layers of agents and public relations people to get his contact information—but she finally got his e-mail address. I sent him a note and mentioned that I had enjoyed meeting him, even if briefly, and would love to get together again for a drink. I told him I was a big fan of his music—and of him personally. We've been friends ever since.

You never know, right?

TAKE IT TO THE TOP

One of my favorite "cold-calling" stories was told to me by my friend Robert Wiesenthal, the chief financial officer of Sony. When Rob was just starting out as an investment banker, during the real estate recession of the early 1990s, he decided to pour a good chunk of his money into a property in the Hamptons. It was a good investment, he thought, even though it was a bit of a financial stretch for him at the time. He was young and just starting out, and his money was limited. He was approved for a construction loan that bridged to a mortgage. He spent his last dime on the land, so his idea was to seek a certificate of occupancy for the house he planned to build and then to pull some money out of the deal.

Rob started building, but eight weeks into construction he still had no formal commitment letter from Dime Savings Bank, the institution that had offered its initial approval on the loan. He called every day for two weeks, until finally he heard from the builders with the distressing news that they were going to stop construction. Finally, with this ultimatum in hand, Rob seemed to make some headway with the Dime loan officer. The guy told him to stand by his fax machine—which Rob took to mean that the commitment letter was on its way. So Rob took the guy at his word. Thirty minutes later, nothing. A couple of hours later, nothing. Rob put in several more calls before the close of business that day, but no one would take his calls or return any of his messages.

Two days later, Rob finally got through to someone at Dime who told him the bank was getting out of the construction loan business. This was certainly a surprising and unwelcome turn. The loan officer on the other end of the phone was very sorry, he said, but Dime could no longer offer Rob the promised financing.

Poor Rob was up against it. His down payment was nonrefundable, and he was already into his builders for their foundation work. If Dime wouldn't come through on its commitment, he would essentially forfeit his life savings, so he sat down and wrote a nasty letter to the bank's CEO, detailing all of Dime's wrongdoings. After reading the letter, he tore it up and wrote another, this time without any nastiness or vitriol. Even at a young age, Rob knew that these types of "scorched earth" approaches to a business deal gone bad can be short-sighted and dangerous. After all, you never know where people end up. On this second pass, he took a more professional approach, making the all-important point that the bank was in the customer service business, and that he too was in the customer service business. "Let me tell you the story of what happened to me," he wrote, "and let me know your thoughts."

The next morning, he walked to Dime's headquarters, off Fifth Avenue, hoping to deliver the letter personally. Back then, there was no real security presence at most midtown offices, and Rob was able to walk past the guards and onto the elevators leading to the executive floor. He was dressed in a suit, carrying an envelope, and probably looked like an executive messenger. He asked for the CEO's office. Dime's CEO at the time, Richard Parsons, would go on to become the CEO of Time Warner and, after that, Citigroup. Rob was of course surprised to hear back personally from anyone, especially Dick Parsons, since he had essentially broken into the man's office. Instead of being furious with him for trespassing, Dick Parsons told Rob that he had appointed himself Rob's loan officer and that he had his loan. They talked for a while and appeared to hit it off. At some point, Dick asked, "By the way, what do you do for a living?"

Rob explained that he was a media analyst, so their talk turned to the media industry. By the end of the call, Rob had more than his loan—he had an influential new friend and a valuable contact. A couple of years later, when Rob called on Time Warner as a banker, Dick of course remembered their first encounter. He asked Rob if he ever paid back the loan. (He did.)

Today, Sony is one of Citi's top investment banking clients—so once again, you never know.

To be sure, Rob's gambit was a bit of a crapshoot. You can't expect to sneak into some corporate office and get a fair hearing. (Frankly, I would never have had the brass even to try!) And I suppose you can't expect to get a response from a prominent businessman like Carlos Slim without a recognizable name like mine. But your stationery doesn't have to say "Trump" for people to read your note, and you certainly don't have to go skulking around in the predawn hours to get your message across. As it is, I hear back from only a small percentage of the high-profile people I contact, and in those cases my name doesn't seem to have as much to do with the response as the time and care I took to reach out in the first place. You'd be surprised at how accessible people can be if you approach them in the right way. Experience tells me that the more successful the individuals, the more likely they are to respond to an unsolicited appeal. After all, they didn't get to be successful by stiff-arming every idea or opportunity or exchange in their path. Plus, I think there's some of that "prettiest girl in school" mystique at the very top rungs of the corporate ladder. Believe it or not, people don't leave that kind of self-defeating attitude in the high school cafeteria. It follows them into their careers as well, in one way or another. That's one reason a lot of aspiring entrepreneurs don't even consider approaching the best and brightest in their field; they don't think it'll get them anywhere. The assumption is that leading innovators are swamped with requests for their time and attention, but that's often not the case. In some ways, people in positions of great power are a lot like the prettiest girl in school. Truth is, you're probably facing much less competition for their time than you might think.

The way I look at it is that these "cold calls" are a no-lose proposition. If there's no response, there's no response. I don't take it personally. I don't expect a response, so I'm never disappointed. The worst-case scenario is that I'll run into someone I've tried to contact at an event and they'll snub me—but so what? I'll just cross that name off my list and move on to the next. Or I'll find another opportunity to reach out a couple of months later and try again, with the same positive energy, enthusiasm, and confidence I put out the first time around.

Be assured that most CEOs won't be as willing to look past an "ambush" as Dick Parsons seemed to be. I can't say for sure how I would have responded if I'd been approached in the same way—somewhere between impressed and spooked, I'm guessing. Most executives are more comfortable within their own little wombs of corporate bureaucracy than they are at connecting directly with people outside their organization. I understand that, and I appreciate it. But I also ignore it from time to time and go for it anyway. I have observed, however, that entrepreneurial types who run their own companies are more likely to open their doors to intelligent, forward-thinking people who are just starting out. It's not just that they enjoy sharing their own experiences, but they also remember how things were for them when they were looking for their first breaks—and they're anxious to keep plugged in to the fresh perspectives offered by the next generation.

I tell people just starting out to keep taking those shots and they'll be surprised at what they get back on the rebound. Warren Buffett, for example, is well known for frequently answering his own phone. How cool would that be, to make a call to Omaha and have Warren Buffett himself pick up and start talking? Up and down the list of our most successful leaders at our most successful companies, you'll find people just like him. They might not answer their own phone, but they just might answer your letter or take your call.

Something to keep in mind, when you're doing the reaching: it's up to you, the person initiating the contact, to keep that dialogue going—especially if the person you're contacting is more senior, more experienced, more important. A lot of young people make an initial effort, they hustle like crazy to get thirty seconds of someone's time, and then they just let things hang there. They check that person off their list as someone they've met and maybe even learned a little something from, but they do nothing to nurture and sustain that relationship. That's a big mistake—or at least another missed opportunity. I'm always working on my network of "relationships," even when there's hardly enough of a connection to call it that.

In other parts of the world, it takes a long time to cultivate a meaningful business relationship. Here in the United States, we'll do business with just about anyone. It's all about the deal and the potential profits. If it makes sense, it's worth pursuing. But almost everywhere else, business is built on trust, and this takes time to cultivate. It's like a dance. I'm constantly looking for a way in, for a next move. Not in a plotting, calculating sort of way, but in a back-of-my-mind, open-ended sort of way. It's all about constantly laying groundwork. I might have made some initial contact or had a brief meeting, but I'm always on the lookout for a reason to make a follow-up call or to send a note that has some meaning to the recipient. Maybe I'll notice an article I think the person might be interested in. Or maybe I'll read that the person just received an award or an honor of some kind. Whatever it is, I'll find a way back in, to keep the conversation going, because if you don't stay in touch and carry things forward, the first contact becomes a useless memory. You can share the story with your friends, but that's about it. It's sure as hell not going to take you anywhere.

FIND THE RIGHT BALANCE

Understand, we didn't really study this type of networking at Wharton. It's just a good habit I fell into early on, and I've kept it up. It wasn't about getting results or cultivating contacts, but it's turned into that over the years. It's yielded some very tangible benefits, and after a while I started to notice that certain approaches work better than others. I'm always careful to stay on the right side of the thin line that runs between enthusiastic and pushy. It's all too easy to fall the wrong way and come across as an annoying young sycophant. You want to be sure you don't present yourself as too anxious, too excited, too *anything.* The best responses tend to come from the most complimentary appeals, as long as those compliments are sincere. Smart people can see through really transparent blowhards in a heartbeat, but that doesn't change the fact that people—even successful, dynamic people—like a good pat on the back. It's human nature. Entrepreneurs love to hear from fresh-faced business school types, telling them they want to model their careers after them. Heartfelt flattery won't get you everywhere in business, but it might get you somewhere, especially when you consider that businesspeople don't usually get fan mail.

At the same time, you want to keep your own ego in check. These notes, phone calls, and artfully arranged chance encounters are not about you; they're about what you can learn by reaching out to the other individual. Don't bog down the conversation with endless chatter about whatever deal you're working on or what you hope to accomplish in your career—unless you're asked. Even then, you'll want to keep your responses simple and straightforward. Be prepared to listen and learn. If you have questions, go ahead and ask them, but not in such a way that it appears you're reading off a list. Let your questions flow naturally from the conversation. Engage. Plug in. And soak up what you can.

If you spend too much time trying to sound clever, you can't possibly sound sincere. Speak from your heart, and tell this person why you admire him or her. Be specific. If you're sending a handwritten note, keep it short and sweet—anything over a page is probably too long, even with an assist from Bob Toll's handy software program. Be sure to sign off with an open-ended invitation to keep the conversation going, but do it in such a way that there's no pressure on the recipient to respond. Then stick the letter in the mail and forget about it.

If you hear back, that's great. If you don't, that's okay too.

When I connected with Carlos Slim, my goal was not to impress him with my command of international finance or Mexican-American relations but to listen to what he had to say about those subjects. If you're lucky enough to get a face-to-face meeting with someone in response to your overture, allow that person to hold court. Let him or her determine the tone and tenor of your conversation. It might be okay to do 80 percent of the talking in a job interview, but this time you'll want to do 80 percent of the listening. Don't spoil your opportunity by trying to prove how smart you are. Nobody cares. If you're truly intelligent and confident, these traits will come across— as long as you don't get in their way. And even if they don't, they're a little beside the point.

Another thing: take the initiative. Take full advantage of the contacts you can make through friends and family, but at the same time be sure you don't take them for granted. It's amazing to me how many young people fail to recognize the tremendous networking opportunities available to them. Obviously, I'm not the only entrepreneur under thirty with the connections to reach out to influential people. I've watched my friends go through entrepreneurial motions of their own, and very few actually make an effort in this area. So many children of privilege and opportunity treat their parents' network of influential friends and contacts like a bequest, but that's hardly the case. Sure, there are many developers and arm's-length acquaintances who might take my call or respond to a note simply out of respect for my family, but that's where it ends. I'm looking to create relationships that are built on something other than a sense of obligation, and I'm careful never to approach any of those influential people from a place of entitlement. If there's any sense of entitlement going on in our exchanges, it's theirs—and they're certainly entitled to ignore me. That's why if I see a flattering article about a developer my father used to do business with, I'll drop him a short note of congratulations. Or if I bump into a lawyer who used to work with my grandfather, I'll try to have a meaningful conversation and be sure to follow up afterward with a handwritten note or an e-mail. That way, if I ever have to call on any of those people for advice or an assist, there'll be a connection that runs deeper than my last name.

I don't limit this type of networking to people I read about in the press. I also make it a point to socialize with bankers, brokers, and other industry types at least twice a week. In this way, I suppose, I believe in casting a wider net than Tony Hsieng. I attend trade events, golf outings, parties, openings—even when I'd rather be spending some quiet time at home or having a fun night out with friends— because this is where business happens. I need to be on the minds of the people I might do business with, people who can introduce me to deal flow and other opportunities. I want to know what they're working on and let them know what I'm working on, in an unobtrusive way, so that they think of the Trump Organization first when they're ready to move a project forward. So that sometimes—more and more, I hope—*they'll* be the ones calling *me*.

My father tells a story that nicely illustrates these points. One night in 1991, with the real estate markets crashing and several banks aggressively seeking repayment of their loans, my father was scheduled to attend a banker's convention at the Waldorf-Astoria in Manhattan. Any other night, he would have gone to the convention without question, but that particular night he was feeling tired and run down from a grueling day of work. He'd been up and at it since sunrise, so he thought he might pass on the event. He actually went home and began to settle in for the night—but then he caught a second wind and thought better of it. He quickly put on his tuxedo and raced over to the Waldorf, just in time for dinner. He'd missed most of the cocktail hour that usually precedes such events, but he contented himself by knowing he'd at least made an appearance.

At dinner, he found himself seated next to a man who didn't seem too interested in talking to him. That happens sometimes, but my father has always been a pretty good dinner table companion. He's charming and fun and smart—all good things. Finally, after about fifteen minutes of his best material, he broke through with the gentleman, and the two began to talk. It was only then that my father recognized the man as one of the bankers seeking to call his loan. My father owed the guy millions! In a room filled with more than a thousand people, my father just happened to be seated next to the one person in a position to help him.

By that point, they'd been getting along well enough, and the banker said, "You know, Donald, you're not such a bad guy. Why don't you come by my office tomorrow and we'll work this thing out?"

Sure enough, that's just what happened. They built on that little piece of common ground they found over dinner and found a way to renegotiate the terms of their loan.

Write the note.

Make the call.

Attend the meeting, the conference, the outing, the party . . .

Whatever it is, make the extra effort. Because, after all, you never know.

BARRY STERNLICHT—Chairman and CEO, Starwood Capital Group

ON DISTINGUISHING YOUR PRODUCT

When you work in a big company, one of the most important things you have to remember is that you are part of a brand. As an employee, you are the embodiment of the brand. You have to put yourself in the brand's position and ask, "How would the brand like me to behave?" The same holds at the top. Every interaction, every initiative, every decision is a branding moment. We're in the hotel business, but I tell our people it's the interactions with the employees that people remember, not the bricks. The hotel can be beautifully designed, but if someone was rude to you while you were there, that's all you talk about when you go home. It helps to be an outsider in the industry. I say that about hotels, but it applies to most situations. I don't want to denigrate hotel schools, but everyone is taught the same thing. It gives you a great base but doesn't help differentiate the product. If every can of Coke tasted different, you wouldn't have a brand. You need the consistency of experience. You have to build a differentiated product. Starting out, you want it to be like Starbucks is to coffee, like Target is to retailing. You have to create an attitude toward the brand, and then you have to enforce it with product innovation and service innovation that distinguish what you're doing from what everyone else is doing.

A lot of my success leading Starwood Hotels & Resorts came in the area of product innovation. We were the smallest of the "big three," as measured by system revenues, trailing Marriott and Hilton, so we needed to be scrappier. We needed to work to find and keep our edge. We became known for our Heavenly Bed. We even did the Heavenly Doggy Bed, and it all stemmed from something I learned in business school, courtesy of Howard Head. He invented Head skis and then turned his attention to tennis and came up with the Prince tennis racket. He said that the most successful inventions are the ones that build on things you use in your everyday life and make them easier, smarter, better. So he took that and applied it to tennis. He stretched the racket head and made a bigger surface. Great idea. He made a huge business out of it. That's what we tried to do with our Heavenly Beds. We took something that people had sort of forgotten about and taken for granted. The trend was to take out costs, and people were trying to save a dollar on their mattresses and pillows and sheets, but if you go back to distinguishing your product and connecting with your consumer, it was a great opportunity. In the hotel business, you can't get any closer to your customer than the bedding. He'll lie on your product for eight or ten hours, so our thought was to put our money back into the bed and build the best bed in the business.

In most businesses, product innovation gives you only a fleeting edge. Anyone can copy what you're doing. But if you can string together a series of innovations, you can be branded as an innovative company. And some of them will stick. The first guy in the space is usually the one who owns it. With MP3 players, Apple made the first big push, so now people think of the iPod. With us, even though Marriott and Hilton and Hyatt all came out with new beds, the Heavenly Bed was Westin's and we earned accolades and market share.

The key to achieving excellence in any organization is to benchmark yourself outside your own industry and to benchmark your company against the best in class—not only in your own industry but all around. Take your human resources, for example, and look for the best human resources in the country, in the world—not just in the hotel industry. Change your standards of excellence, and don't be afraid to do things a little differently. Then, when you look at the benchmarks, find a way to apply them to your business. That's why it's been so helpful that I've come from a different place. It frees you up so you can focus on the centers of differentiating excellence, to distinguish what you're doing from what everybody else in your space is doing.

One of our best innovations came from one of our associates in Canada who happened to notice a curved shower rod in a small bathroom supply catalogue. It was a simple little item that cost only about $13, but it opened up a whole lot of space inside a crowded shower. It made the interior shower space seem much bigger. We took a look at it and very quickly made it one of our standards, but of course everyone else picked up on it. All the other hotels had straight shower rods, and they copied us. It's something that seemed obvious, but someone noticed it, our systems captured the idea, it made it to my desk, and then we implemented it. We had an edge for a while, but it was just one in a series of constant changes needed to keep our brand at the top and relevant. That's when a big company works best, when ideas from the field get to the top without being killed along the way. When the experiences of your customers and your staff have a chance to make your product a little better each day to help you make a difference. Differentiation builds brand value, and brands create economic advantage and therefore sustainable shareholder value.

ELEVEN

GOING IT ALONE

The most courageous act is still to think for yourself.
—EDWARD DE BONO

Behind every new venture there's a certain amount of arrogance and bluster, some version of the notion that you can build a better mousetrap than the other guy—or, in my case, that you can design and market a mousetrap with every conceivable amenity to ensure that the discerning mouse will want to be trapped in upmarket luxury. Whatever it is you're looking to do or make or sell, you build your business on the assumption that you can do it better, smarter, and more efficiently than the competition. Otherwise, what's the point?

I'd been at the Trump Organization for about two years when I came upon an unexpected opportunity to exercise some of these impulses—in an area I hadn't thought to consider. Realize, I wasn't actively looking for a new venture, but I believe you have to keep your feelers out there and pick up whatever signals come your way. It's the spirit of enterprise. This doesn't mean you have to limit your focus to opportunities in your field or your perceived area of expertise. Over the years, my father had made successful forays into what were at the time completely new territories for him—beauty pageants, books, modeling agencies—and I could see the adrenaline rush he'd get from taking a calculated risk and pushing the envelope of his own experience. I'd look

221

on and think, Someday, Ivanka, you'll get your chance. That chance presented itself in a sidelong way. I was pursuing a lead on a piece of land in Fort Myers, Florida. I didn't like the deal when it was laid out for me, but I looked closely at it just the same. Back then, a year or two into my stint at the Trump Organization, I analyzed everything I could get my hands on to educate myself on every aspect of our many businesses, and it was a good thing that I did, because even though this particular property held no real appeal, it led directly to another opportunity.

Specifically, it led to a good working relationship with the young businessman, Moshe Lax, who brought it to me. All business comes down to relationships, at some point or other, and we do well to cultivate them wherever we can. It's been one of the great themes of this first phase of my career, just as it's been one of the great themes of these pages. You never know when a key contact can help you unlock your next great opportunity, and that's what happened. During the next several months, I established a professional friendship with Moshe and his late father Chaim. The three of us got to talking. Even though we'd come together on a real estate proposition, the family's primary business was diamonds. In fact, they owned a substantial diamond manufacturing company based in New York and Israel. Their company was one of the largest vendors of loose diamonds to some of the leading luxury brands in the industry. Moshe was looking to take his business to a whole new level. In that way, I suppose, we were a lot alike, trying to make our own way along a path set out for us by our fathers and trying to extend that path in exciting new directions, which I guess explains why we hit it off.

My new associate was an entrepreneur through and through. I admired that about him. He also wasn't willing to rest on his father's accomplishments or the success of the family business. I admired that as well. In addition to his diamond business and his real estate portfolio, he'd also owned several successful New York City restaurants, so he had some good retail experience to complement his wholesale diamond-cutting background. At the time, he was struggling to get some kind of toehold in retail for his family's diamond business—specifically, he had a storefront on Madison Avenue that wasn't quite performing to his expectations. Try as he might, he couldn't seem to get the design or the branding to work in such a way that he could distinguish his pieces from those made by the jewelry designers located on either side of his boutique. His pieces were meticulously crafted with beautiful diamonds and the finest materials, but they were generic, forgettable. They looked like everything else. There was nothing to bring customers into his nondescript store—and certainly nothing to get them to come back a second or third time.

It made sense that he was struggling, but at the same time it also made sense to push ahead, considering the huge edge he had over other jewelers with his family diamond business. The advantage came in owning his diamond inventory, which essentially made him his own supplier. Moshe therefore believed in the viability of his business and was thinking those stops and starts were just growing pains, something to get past.

We talked through a bunch of ways he might invigorate his jewelry collection, and he sparked to a lot of my ideas. Frankly, so did I. I hadn't realized I had a passion or flair for this type of marketing effort, but I guess I'd flipped through enough fashion magazines and worn enough high-end jewelry to know what might work in this area. Plus, I love and appreciate fine jewelry! What girl doesn't? Especially the daughter of Ivana Trump!

Without realizing it, I found myself getting excited about the prospects of what a recharged jewelry business might look like with me involved in a hands-on way. My new friend recognized that I was both enthusiastic and positioned to bring a singular skill set to his operation, so we started talking about how we might work together on a retail venture. It's not as if either one of us was pursuing the other to do a deal. The talks simply evolved organically over the course of our other business discussions, and the more we looked at opportunities, the more we found a lot to like about the idea of partnering.

FOLLOW YOUR CURIOSITY

A lot of times, when you're looking for opportunities, the best ideas have a way of announcing themselves. As an entrepreneur, you have to be open to what's in front of you. That doesn't mean you don't scour the planet for interesting, off-the-radar deals, but it's a compelling reminder that very often the most viable, most lucrative endeavors are close at hand. As I said, I'd never really thought all that much about the luxury jewelry market until Moshe and I started talking about it, but it seemed like a good fit. My potential partner had great experience in diamonds and tremendous leverage and buying power that would drastically reduce the amount of start-up capital we'd need to launch a new venture. (The traditional barrier to entry for any jeweler working with diamonds is the cost of the diamonds themselves, and we had a ready supply of quality stones at reasonable prices.) For my part, I had a strong background in brand development, which was what the diamond group sorely needed to make a name for itself at the retail level. Plus I had some experience and plenty of contacts in design and fashion, in addition to a lot of exciting ideas for a collection that would truly stand out.

In all, there seemed to be a buildable, sustainable business there for the taking, so we took our conversations to the next level. As we did, I started to realize that I'd been hungering for an opening to make my mark *outside* our core family business. It hadn't been any kind of front-burner passion, but it was there, deep down, in a stomach-grumbling sort of way. I was doing well at Trump and in just a couple of years had managed to silence most of the people who'd assumed I was there on my name and my bloodline, but it can be a great and validating thing to strike out on your own in a venture that has nothing to do with your famous father, so I responded to that aspect of a potential partnership as well. Of course, my primary interest and responsibility would remain at Trump, but there was no reason to stiff-arm such an appealing sideline opportunity.

Understand, I wasn't looking to merely bankroll a new business. That had no appeal to me at that stage in my career—not to mention that it just wasn't practical. I certainly didn't have the kind of money to underwrite someone else's dreams. I realize, of course, that this is often the end game for a lot of investors and silent partner types, but I was in no position to invest in someone else's business. I *was*, however, willing to invest in a dream of my own, and very quickly the jewelry idea emerged as a kind of passion. It sent me back to so many long-ago evenings, sitting watching my mother as she got dressed for some gala or other. I used to love watching her pick out her jewelry. She'd let me try on all the different pieces, and I'd vamp and pose in front of the mirror, imagining that I looked so elegant, so sophisticated. It made me feel so grown up. She used to take me shopping with her, too, although the venerable jewelry shops on Madison and Fifth Avenues tended to feel like cold mausoleums to a little girl. Very often, my mother and I would be the only customers in the store, and I remember feeling as if all employees' eyes were on me, watching my every move. (They probably thought I would swipe something!) In reality, they were all fixed on my mother, willing her to make a major purchase.

Personally, I found all that scrutiny somewhat oppressive. Intimidating. The people who worked in these stores were always so solicitous of my mother and the few other customers who came in, but I never felt entirely comfortable in such an austere environment, which I guess explained why I never stepped into those stores on my own. It's not that I couldn't afford to treat myself to a beautiful new necklace or a lovely pair of earrings from time to time, but I just wasn't drawn to that type of shopping experience, and neither were my peers.

In my discussions with Moshe, I started to think there might be a way to turn that disconnect to advantage.

BUILD A BRAND

The more I thought back on my mother's experiences in those high-end stores and my once-removed experiences at her side, the more I recognized an opportunity for a luxury jewelry line created for modern women based on their lifestyle needs and tastes, women who weren't waiting around for their husbands or fathers to buy them a fine piece of jewelry as a gift. Women who had a sense of flair and fashion that perhaps wasn't being reflected in the designs of some of the more traditional, high-end jewelers. Women who weren't comfortable wearing their grandmother's jewelry but who wanted to invest in fresher, more vibrant heirloom chic pieces that they would enjoy wearing for a long time and really take pleasure in, before passing them on to their own children or grandchildren. And above all, women who were perhaps looking for guidance from their more fashion-forward daughters on what to wear—as opposed to looking to their mothers, which had been the case for generations.

As we kicked things around, I realized there was a void in the marketplace waiting to be filled, so we struck a partnership deal and set about filling it. Moshe already had a location on Madison Avenue, so our first move was to close the store and redesign the whole space from top to bottom. We hired a great design team to handle our makeover, which would extend to our packaging as well. Our initial goal was to give the store itself a distinctive, art deco look that would be warmer and more inviting than the mausoleum model I remembered as a kid. The look would be reinforced by the aesthetic of our pieces, as we began developing the collection, but the first order of business was retrofitting the space and creating a signature style, identity, and logo for our emerging brand.

Along the way, I made some mental notes on what we'd need to do as we introduced our collection, and I share them here for the way they apply to the launch of any new business, product, or service:

Do a comprehensive trademark search. This is an obvious first step, but you'd be surprised how many start-ups hit a wall when it turns out someone else already owns their brand name. In our dot-com age, this means you'll have to secure the accompanying domain name as well.

Develop a powerful identifier. Your look and logo are incredibly important. These days, your Web site design is also a part of that "look" (check out www.ivankatrumpcollection.com), along with your packaging and collateral materials. Spend some time on these, because they'll be the image that goes home with your customers, whether or not they make a purchase or sign on to your service. Be memorable.

Do not confuse supply with demand. Another basic. Just because you have an item in plenty doesn't necessarily mean a lot of people will want to buy it. Identify the demand for your product first, and then dive in. Luxury condos offer a great case in point. Developers will pitch a site as ideal simply because other developers are building similar projects on the abutting properties. But we're not talking Field of Dreams here. "If you build it, they will come" might be a powerful message in a tear-jerker baseball movie, but an overdeveloped resort area can be a huge negative.

Identify the void in your market, and position your brand so that you uniquely fill it. If you mean to provide a product or service that's currently unavailable at your planned price point, be sure to know your competition at the high and low ends. There might be a reason no one is trafficking in that unclaimed middle. If not, find it, and fill it.

Create a strong and consistent identity. Whatever you want your image to be, establish it early and stay true to your identity. Without an established reputation, you don't have a brand, so take pains to keep on point and on message. Otherwise, you'll miss your target. For example, Trump is synonymous with luxury, glamour, and elegance. Every project we undertake reinforces that reputation. To deviate from these principles would undermine our brand's values.

Define your market. This one's basic. Figure out who your target customer is, even if it's not obvious at the outset. The better you know your customers and their needs, the more easily you can sell to them.

Make sure your team understands your mission, your vision, your objectives. You'd be surprised how many salespeople I meet who don't understand their own product or share their boss's vision. At our hotels, we have a two-day acclimation program to thoroughly explain to our new hires who we are and what the Trump Hotel Collection stands for. Get your team on board, or you'll have a team of free agents moving to their own agendas.

Focus on customer service. In a competitive market, every business is a service business. The customer is always, always, always right. Even when he or she is wrong. Be sure to put a system into place that gives your customer a voice—and, just as important, be sure to listen to it. The CEO of Orient Express hotels randomly connects to three rooms across the portfolio each day, introducing himself and asking guests how they're enjoying their stays. Do the math: three calls, 365 days a year . . . that's a lot of feedback.

Foster brand loyalty at every opportunity. One of the indicators of our success on the real estate front is that we have many condominium owners who buy units in more than one Trump building. We nurture these relationships and make sure our repeat buyers know that we value their business by giving them a first look at some of our properties in presales, supporting their philanthropic initiatives, or perhaps even offering them accommodations in one of our hotel properties. Whatever it takes to keep them coming back.

Hold off spending whenever possible. You need to spend money to make money. This is especially true when launching your new brand, but if you're not careful you'll find that the majority of your expenditures will have minimal impact on your success. Do your research first, before spending heavily in any one area. Look closely at your product design, your target segments, and your marketing strategy—then allocate your money to where it will do the most good.

I'm not a big believer in hiring consultants. My style is to talk to as many different people as I can, to pick the brain of every industry expert I have access to, and then make my own decision. Very often, when you reach out to the right people, you'll collect the advice you need for free, and when it's freely given, it strikes a more resonant chord. I'd much rather hear from a friend or a professional acquaintance with an honest opinion on a matter she knows something about than a hired consultant who might simply sell me on her own agenda, espouse conventional wisdom, or tell me what she thinks I want to hear.

So I reached out to everyone I knew in the jewelry industry. I talked to diamond merchants, vendors, retail investors, everyone I could get to sit still and let me pepper them with questions. I asked them which strategies had been the most successful for them and which had proven ineffective. I also spoke to women who would make up our target market, to get a sense of what they were looking for. I spoke to my friends, but also to my mother and quite a few of her friends as well. I really tried to cover a lot of ground, and everything I kept hearing was that people were looking for a distinctive luxury jewelry line to bridge the gap between what they'd grown up wearing and what their mothers wore.

Basically, I embarked on a long, informal "gut check," and here's what my gut told me: For generations, men did an overwhelming majority of the shopping in the luxury jewelry market. Or at least they signed off on most purchases. Their wives and girlfriends let it be known what they wanted—sometimes without a whole lot of subtlety—and then the men went out and made the purchase. Usually, the sale was tied to some occasion or other, such as a birthday or anniversary. But times had changed to where women were now making most of these purchases for themselves up to a certain price point, so it made sense that our store should reflect this shift. Some of the world's leading jewelers had made a passing effort to at least acknowledge the power of the independent female shopper, yet most had not really responded to this change in the marketplace. They were still doing business the old-fashioned way, so we set out to create a female-friendly atmosphere, one that would effectively and comfortably empower women to take charge of this aspect of their lives. They might still drop hints to their husbands or boyfriends that they're eyeing this or that special piece for Valentine's Day, but during the course of the year they might also drop in and pick up something for themselves. I realized that there was a whole generation of women out there like myself, who wanted to reward themselves for their hard work and accomplishments—and somehow could do so with my jewelry!

Consider these numbers: 90 percent of our decision makers are women; 50 percent buy for themselves; and 40 percent make the selection and simply direct their husbands to our store to close the actual purchase. Thus, although 50 percent of our in-store customers might be male, in reality male decision makers account only for around 10 percent of our business. (The rest are just doing what they're told!)

Why not model our product and retail environment to women and to their wants and needs? Other jewelry stores are traditionally masculine, most likely because the vast majority of diamond retailers are male: Laurence Graff, Louis Cartier, Harry Winston, and so on. But my gut and my contacts kept telling me to keep the store romantic, fresh, inviting. We wanted to turn it into a bright, lively, warm environment. We retained all of the sumptuousness of the classic Fifth Avenue jeweler, with lots of mirrors and silk, rich crown moldings, and the finest marble, but we looked to shed the snobby, elitist tones. One way to do this, we thought, was to accent the space with art deco patterns and pops of color. After a whole lot of reflection and consideration we selected coral as our "signifier" color and worked it in to the design. (More on this in a moment.) We also decided to serve champagne and hot chocolate because we wanted a visit to our boutique to be a fun, carefree experience. It would still feel like a superluxurious environment when you stepped inside, but also as if you were entering a woman's dressing room or boudoir. The effect was a whole lot softer and more welcoming than you might expect.

One of the simplest innovations to our space turned out to be one of the most meaningful. In Manhattan, most luxury jewelry boutiques feature a "man-trap" vestibule at the front of the store. That's the double-door entryway you see that essentially traps customers between the door to the street and a second door into the store itself, as a security measure. Customers have to wait to be buzzed in through each door, so no one can race into or out of the store without being eyeballed by security staff. It serves a purpose, I suppose, but I found it so institutional, so offputting. It establishes a kind of haughty tone before the customer even crosses your threshold. Of course, when you have millions of dollars of shopliftable merchandise on the other side of the entrance, you and your insurance company might welcome the extra layer of protection. That said, we figured we could accomplish the same goal with our full-time security guards positioned at the store entrance—and dressed nonthreateningly as doormen. We would also have our guards welcome our clients as they opened the door, and offer a personal greeting—the first sign that their shopping experience would be different at our store. At first, our insurers weren't so crazy about our doorman idea, because they were accustomed to dealing with the problem in a set way, but we were able to prevail and in this way helped to establish a softer, more inviting tone, quite literally from the moment the customer stepped into the store.

Next we started to pay attention to our target market and our price structure. We wanted to offer luxurious pieces in the five-, and six-, and even seven-figure range, but at the same time we wanted to offer entry-level pieces priced between $500 and $1,000. That's a pretty wide spectrum. Granted, our lower-priced pieces would still represent a major purchase for most people and certainly more than you would spend at Tiffany & Co. for an entry-level item, but we believed this was appropriate for our target customers. This way, young women making their first significant purchases could grow with our brand as they grew in buying power. At Tiffany, of course, customers could make the same lifelong connection, but as I studied their product I realized a lot of their resources were focused on selling items that cost hundreds of dollars, not thousands. Since Tiffany does that so well, I didn't want to compete in the same space. We wanted to fill that void just below the high-end diamond jewelers such as Harry Winston, Bulgari, Graff, Van Cleef & Arpels—the boutiques that exemplified acquisitions of $50,000 or more—while at the same time creating luxurious pieces that would be the envy of any jeweler. That was the market we were after, with a few little items sprinkled in at $500 or $600 that were consistent with our higher-priced pieces. As a fine jeweler, all of the pieces in our collection, from entry level to high end, were handcrafted in 18K white gold, platinum, and diamonds. That meant focusing on beautiful accents like seed pearls and black onyx, as opposed to diamonds, in our moderately priced pieces. (Later on, we would add lines in 18K rose and yellow gold, using diamonds along with rock crystal and other gemstones.) The idea was to create an environment for our younger, less affluent customers to enter the universe of our brand with fun but meaningful purchases while they aspire to some of our more luxurious pieces—all without sacrificing any quality or prestige on the way up and without sacrificing the image we were cultivating for ourselves as the innovative and inspired jeweler for women.

It's important to note here that every decision we made in this launch phase of our business was with an eye toward a seismic shift in American consumer culture and the role women now play in it. This, too, went into the gut-check category of insights and information I was able to collect and process in my "due diligence" phase. I came to realize that it no longer made sense to build a luxury boutique around the idea of trapping a wealthy man in your store and essentially bully- ing him into making a large purchase. Ten, twenty, thirty years ago, customers didn't have access to all the information that's so readily available today. They couldn't go online and compare designs and prices. Today, if they're not blown away by a particular piece or are turned off by a shopping experience, they'll just go elsewhere. People do their homework as never before, so I couldn't let it worry me if someone left our store without making a purchase.

What *would* worry me was if they didn't come back.

DEVELOP A SIGNATURE

One of our first and foremost needs was a name. We had to call our- selves . . . something. An obvious choice, if we were looking to build and sustain a brand, was my own name. After all, if I was going to be the public face of our jewelry collection, it made good business sense to reinforce that connection in the name of our line. Indeed, the only real debate we had internally was whether to use my full name or just my first name. Looking back, I think my first name would have worked quite nicely, being that it is very distinctive. But we all realized that if we were looking to expand into an international market, it would be a huge missed opportunity to leave the Trump name on the cutting room floor, so to speak. I'd seen first-hand the value our Trump brand brought to saleable real estate, so it made sense to reach for it here as well.

For that reason, we never really looked at a word or a phrase to denote the luxury and opulence of our line—such as "Luster" or "Brilliance"—because those kinds of descriptive names seemed more midmarket than high end. Plus, most of the established, classic jewelers in the world stood behind a family name or the name of their founder, so it made sense to use my name, as well—a name that already represented luxury, glamour, wealth, and aspiration. After only a little bit of back-and-forth, we settled on "Ivanka Trump." To our thinking, it was a value-added proposition—especially now, with the higher profile I enjoy from being at my father's side on *The Apprentice*. There was built-in name recognition so it'd be foolish to set my birthright aside in favor of something generic.

After naming ourselves, we had to decide on the color of our brand—and here it was another no-brainer. My two favorite colors are coral and blue. Tiffany had claimed robin's egg blue, so that left coral, which was fine with me. It reminded me of my childhood in Palm Beach—my mother's house was awash in that color. Coral was soft, feminine, inviting, distinctive—all good things—but it's also vibrant, strong, and full of personality. The more we looked at it, the more we realized that coral would do a lot of business for us and set the right tone for our brand. Our interior designers worked it into the look of our store, even as we would work it into the designs of our pieces and our packaging.

Most important: it was *available*. Cartier had its distinctive blood red. Asprey had its trademark purple. Van Cleef, yellow. But coral was wide open, so we put it to work for us as a highlight feature in our store design, our jewelry designs, and the design of our packaging.

That powerful signifier I wrote about earlier? The color coral would be ours, and you can find it as a detail element on the back of many of our most popular items. I love the way it peeks out of the back of one of our earrings or the clasp of a necklace, like a wonderful, unexpected surprise. Our idea was for people to see coral on a piece of jewelry and think immediately of Ivanka Trump—a design trigger like the red sole of a Christian Louboutin shoe. It's instantly recognizable and great branding.

A word on packaging. It's a big deal. Once again, think Tiffany: that blue box is almost as important as the piece it contains, because the box itself makes a powerful statement. It's ubiquitous and memorable. In some respects, the company pays as much attention to controlling its packaging inventory as it does its merchandise—and it should, because the box is the key to the brand. In the engagement ring segment of the jewelry business, for example, the designs tend to be fairly straightforward and simple. People look for classic, timeless pieces, which means that a ring purchased in one store can look a lot like a ring purchased in another store. A would-be groom on a budget could probably go to Forty-seventh Street in Manhattan and buy a comparable ring for a lot less from a mom-and-pop-type storefront jeweler, and no one would ever know the difference once it's on his fiancée's finger, but that's not the crucial moment of the transaction. It's the moment the ring is offered when you want it to make a statement, and we've been conditioned to think that the same-seeming engagement ring has to be presented in that iconic blue Tiffany box, so I'm sure there are a lot of guys out there who'd jump to buy a generic ring in the Diamond District if they could somehow place it in a Tiffany package.

With this in mind, then, we spent a lot of time on our own packaging, and in the end we came up with a breathtakingly lovely box, to accent our pieces in a memorable way—and to announce them as keepsakes before the box is even opened. It's a gorgeous white enamel box lined with black velvet, with a signifier "IT" clasp. The box itself can be displayed on a nightstand or bureau—and many of our clients do just that.

The name, the packaging, the warm and friendly in-store environment—all of this was just marketing. In the end our success would come down to the strength of our collection, so we directed most of our energies there. The abiding impulse was to update the classic deco look and to avoid anything that might come across as too trendy or ephemeral. Trendy is a dangerous label for a luxury jewelry line, because you want the pieces to endure the test of time. People don't want to spend a substantial amount of money on a piece of jewelry that might be out of style next season, especially in a down economy. One of the phrases we kept kicking around in our strategy sessions was "heirloom chic." What that meant, to us, was that we'd be classic but with a twist. We offered a lot of black and white in our first collection because it seemed so youthful, so vibrant, yet at the same time you can't get much more traditional and pure than designs with a black and white contrast.

We chose a simple oval as our proprietary shape, another brand signifier, and tried to incorporate it into our designs wherever appropriate. Here again, we were out to establish a look, one we hoped would become instantly recognizable as an Ivanka Trump piece. No other high-end jeweler had seized on the shape in such an identifying way—plus, it's such a graceful, elegant symbol, don't you think? It's so feminine, so vital, and it lends itself beautifully to some distinctive earring and jewelry designs.

My goal, really, was to reinvent the classic Hollywood-type jewelry from a bygone era but to update the look so it wasn't so heavy and dated. A lot of antique pieces from my grandmother's era seem antiquated today, so I wanted to design something a bit cleaner, a bit more elegant—a contemporary take on a classic aesthetic. Also, "wearability" was a key factor in our design. My brand is targeted at the modern woman, who wears her jewelry day into night—not as a status symbol but as an expression of her style and personality.

As our tagline suggests, we wanted to "rock tradition."

More and more, as we jumped through all the hoops that stood in our path along our start-up course, I found myself channeling my mother. Her attention to detail, from back in her Plaza days, was now mine. I'd catch myself obsessing over the tiniest detail.

As I write this, it's too soon to tell how much long-term success we might find with the Ivanka Trump Collection. As of now, in this tough economy, we're doing very well. We've been featured in major fashion magazines such as *Vogue, Elle,* and *Harper's Bazaar.* We've won awards for our innovative Web site design. And, we've attracted a wide range of celebrity clients such as Demi Moore, Mary Louise Parker, Alicia Keys, and Rihanna who beautifully "advertise" our collection every time they wear one of our pieces.

In just a short time, we've developed a solid and loyal following. Actually, we're doing better than "very well," and we're building a strong brand identity in the luxury segment of our industry. We're constantly working on new designs and looking to expand into additional locations.

For the time being, though, we've succeeded beyond my wildest expectations. By every measure, we're up and running. And we're making a name for ourselves—*my* name!—in a field so far removed from my father's sphere of influence that it feels utterly my own.

PUTTING IT ALL TOGETHER

Never, never, never give up.

—WINSTON CHURCHILL

Synergy. It's one of the most overused terms in business, but it's at the heart of every successful endeavor, and as I look back on the career I've jump-started at the Trump Organization, I realize it's at the heart of everything I've done as well.

So indulge me over these final few pages while I wear out the term a little bit more and offer a prime example of the synergy at play in my own career. During the 2009 season of *Celebrity Apprentice,* I managed to integrate my role at the Trump Organization with my television persona in such a way that it reinforced my jewelry brand. That's a triple whammy on the synergy front, and it happened in a seamless way. You see, one of the hallmarks of my father's television show has been the brand-backed tasks or projects the contestants are assigned. These invariably involve a corporate sponsor, which naturally looks to integrate its product or service into our story line so that there's a clear carryover benefit to its business. Think of it as a transparent form of product placement, but you can be sure that NBC and the show's producers (including my father, naturally) are being compensated handsomely for the "free" airtime. A sixty-second commercial during a hit prime-time network show can run into millions of dollars, and we're offering exposure in the form of product integration that can sometimes stretch across an entire episode.

To be sure, some of the *Apprentice* tasks are sponsor-free (such as the time contestants had to operate a bicycle rickshaw business in midtown Manhattan), and occasionally there are last-minute opportunities to fill a sudden hole in our production schedule when a planned sponsor falls away for one reason or another. When this happens, I'll sometimes suggest a replacement idea, and here I looked to create an opportunity for my jewelry line by pitching a segment that would feature some of our pieces in a competitive fashion show and auction environment. The idea was to pit the two teams of celebrities, which at that point in the show included the poker player Annie Duke, Melissa Rivers, and *Playboy* model Brande Roderick on one side and Joan Rivers, Clint Black, and Hershel Walker on the other side. (Walker, incidentally, used to play football for my father's New Jersey Generals United States Football League franchise.) The teams would have to select several pieces from my collection and then auction them off at a big charity event. Whoever raised the most money through their auction efforts would win the task—and survive for at least another week on the show.

The producers liked my pitch. It offered a very entertaining story line and the chance for the celebrity contestants to demonstrate their abilities in areas such as sales, marketing, promotion, and management—which of course was the object of an effective *Apprentice* task. After all, we're putting the contestants' business skills on display, so the idea is to develop a project that covers the gamut. This one seemed to fit the bill. As an added bonus, it had the television-friendly elements of fashion, charity, and glamour, all rolled into a business setting. It turned out that the producers liked the idea so much, they turned it into a two-hour special episode.

More important for me personally, the episode offered a great way to integrate the three aspects of my career—we even shot a segment inside my Madison Avenue boutique. You can't put a price on that kind of exposure. Plus, our jewelry line was discussed throughout the entire episode, and several of our pieces were featured prominently— with each of the remaining celebrities taking turns marveling at how beautiful they were!

When you roll up your sleeves and set to work in a bunch of different areas, you can't help but help yourself. Within our hotel collection, to highlight another example, I'll sometimes offer our most loyal and valuable guests a $500 credit toward a jewelry purchase in my boutique (or on our Web site)—as a way of saying thank you to our best customers and at the same time driving the right kind of traffic into the store. Or I'll take a potential development partner or important banking contact out for a round of golf and a wonderful lunch at one of our Trump International courses to help seal a deal. It's a way of networking and relationship building that exposes that person to the quality of life available to all Trump associates.

Call it what you will—but I call it synergy. Everything I've done has led directly to what I'm doing, just as everything I'm doing is tied in to what I might do next. It's all of a piece, and it's the same way with my father and brothers—my mother, too, now that she's off doing her own thing. After all, we don't work in a vacuum. And we don't live in one, either, which is why I often think the best approach to life and career is to reach for everything that makes sense and hold on to what works.

As guiding principles go, you could do worse.